THE SCANDAL OF VIRGINIA GREY

THE SCANDAL OF VIRGINIA GREY

ISBN: 978-1-966442-41-7

The book you are about to read deals, in part, with the topic of suicide. If you or a loved one are struggling with thoughts of suicide, please call the **Suicide and Crisis Lifeline by dialing 988.**

CONTENTS

"The Scandal of Virginia Grey"

A Fiction Based on True Events

by Wendy Crane

*V*irginia closed her eyes, swallowed hard and took a deep breath to calm her present state of anxiety. Never before had she felt so vulnerable as she did at this very moment—Lying face up on a table in the dimly lit room, her naked body covered only by a bed sheet, and the very strong and capable hands of the woman she and her husband betrayed tightly gripping her neck...

CHAPTER 1

Pure Joy

Virginia Novak, born Virginia Abigail Grey, grew up in a small village in New York's Hudson Valley. Virginia was named after her maternal Grandmother (Granny), and while somewhat old-fashioned, Virginia treasured her namesake. Virginia's nickname, coined by family and close friends, was Ginny or Gin for short. Even though Granny passed away when Virginia was a teenager, she always had the most precious memories of spending time at Granny's house—playing in her old cottage house, pretending it was a magical castle filled with all sorts of mythical characters and beasts and even a secret treasure hidden in a chest guarded by a fire-breathing dragon. The treasure just so happened to be a drawer of candy that Granny kept stocked full in her dining room buffet cabinet.

Virginia loved the sound of laughter as her parents and grandparents played the card game, Pinochle, at the kitchen table;

the creaking of the old wooden staircase as she walked upstairs; the smell of White Rain hairspray and Jergens hand lotion in Granny's bedroom; the taste of real churned butter on freshly baked bread; and the sound of the grandfather clock ticking as Virginia snuggled up and put her head on Granny's lap on the olive-green sofa to take a nap. Granny's home was a happy place. A place of safety and innocence. So, Virginia bore the name proudly in honor of Granny and the fond memories she carried with her.

Virginia was not a "planned" pregnancy, nor did her parents desire to have any more children, as they already had three who were evenly spaced at two years apart. And then, to their surprise, seven years later, would come another. Upon hearing the news of her pregnancy, Mama Grey cried, albeit not tears of gladness. Just one year prior, her father was tragically killed in a motorcycle accident. It was a horrific incident, leaving Mama Grey with a sense of great sudden loss. So, upon learning of her pregnancy, she was still emotionally raw after her father's death and didn't think she could handle having another baby. Given the timing, however, she surmised that even though she didn't want to have more children, she felt God gave Virginia to her as a gift to help her through her season of grief. Thus, she named her new unexpected baby girl Virginia (meaning "pure") and Abigail (meaning "my father's joy"). Virginia became Mama Grey's pure joy that followed her season of weeping.

Growing up, Virginia was a shy yet active little girl. Since her siblings were much older and were off doing their own thing most of the time, she became a loner—very independent with a creative, sensitive soul. She'd often spend her days, weather permitting, playing outside, going for bike rides, swimming, or tumbling in the yard practicing her gymnastics routines. But on rainy days, you'd often find Virginia closed off in her bedroom, writing plays or songs and then secretly performing them in front of an audience of stuffed animals.

Life in the Grey home wasn't always perfect. There were, of course, good times and bad times, but as Virginia grew older, she came to appreciate the Christian values and belief system that her parents instilled. It was the constant variable through whatever life threw their way. When fear and doubt arose, they chose to believe. When money was tight, they chose to be generous. When quarrels and tempers erupted, they chose to love. When they needed direction, healing, or help, they prayed.

Virginia knew that kind of faith did not come easily—it was hewn through trials and suffering. She realized the "walking twelve miles to school in the snow, uphill both ways" kind of adversity engrained a measure of steadfastness and attitude of thankfulness in her parents that Virginia admired greatly. She hoped to have that kind of faith someday. She would find, however, that in order for her to experience that deep faith, she would first have to face her crisis of faith that would inevitably come knocking.

While Virginia was very pretty and well-liked, she didn't take to the dating scene much, struggling with insecurity and low self-esteem throughout her life. It was obvious to her that she didn't measure up to the perfect 10s plastered on TV and magazines, and she didn't possess that hourglass figure or have that pearly white smile. She also held true to the standard of sexual purity and waiting for "Mr. Right." There were those who voiced their concern about her lack of an active dating life and even questioned her sexual orientation, as she spent a lot of time with a female friend at the time. Annoyed at hearing this chatter, Virginia assured them she was not a lesbian… just a woman in waiting… and she hadn't found the right guy yet, or he hadn't found her. But as time went on, the sense of loneliness and desiring a husband grew steadily intense.

By age 27, Virginia was thriving in her career as a paralegal in one of the most prestigious law firms in New York City. She saved some money to rent a small but charming Brownstone apartment in the Upper West Side, only a short walk away from Central Park. She loved going for long walks and frequenting nearby coffee shops for her customary honey latte, so this was the perfect location for Virginia. Plus, it was a short drive to her family's home in Sleepy Hollow. When she wasn't working, she spent most of her free time at church, volunteering or attending music rehearsals and mid-week Bible classes. Church was energizing for Virginia. A place of safety, encouragement, community, and belonging. Unfortunately, a series of events was about to topple her sanctuary.

Virginia's local church was preparing for a special meeting the following day, and there were a few leaders and volunteers gathered in a circle to pray in the church offices adjacent to the meeting room. In the days preceding, Virginia had been dealing with some relational issues that troubled her deeply, in part from her own doing, involving one of the attorneys in the office—the tall, dark, and handsome type. The type that didn't adhere to boundaries. He had been showing a great deal of attention to Virginia, frequently stopping by her desk to talk, asking her to go out with some colleagues for after-work drinks. His persistent advancements became a source of flattery for Virginia wherein she found herself giving into the flirtation, despite his marital status. Her inner voice of conviction weighed heavily on her, and she felt shameful for how she felt about his attention. For days, she had been crying out to God for forgiveness and strength to overcome the situation, placing her brokenness at his feet. She was praying for a spiritual encounter but had no clue about the phenomenon that was soon to occur.

As their hands connected and hearts stilled, the worship song, "Father, I want you to hold me," played quietly in the background. Suddenly, something happened. There was no way to coordinate such an experience. No way to conjure up such a move of the

Spirit. But God revealed Himself in that very simple moment. The Father of all creation became Father to Virginia in a very tangible way that evening. In response, she fell to her knees and began to sob uncontrollably. She knew she was in the Presence of the One who knew her completely... and yet loved her unreservedly! The holiness of that moment was indescribable. She felt cleansed.

Over a period of months, the Father continued His Holy work. While Virginia considered herself a Christian her whole life, she felt as though she was born again "again" during this time. Even though she did not have a terrible earthly example of a father that tainted her perception of God the Father, there were aspects of her relationship with Daddy Grey—certain characteristics of fatherhood—that she unintentionally projected heavenward and adopted into her belief system. During this outpouring of the Father's Heart, she came to recognize the misconceptions she held—that God the Father was angry with her when she was not perfect or that, somehow, she just didn't "measure up" in His eyes, or that her femininity was flawed. It was a time of profound healing for Virginia as she came to experience the goodness of God on a much deeper level than she had ever known. The following week, there were some changes in the office dynamics, as a position in the real estate law division opened up, and management asked her to transfer from the litigation team to fill in. This meant working on a completely different floor, away from the attorney with whom she had been struggling. It wasn't a fix for Virginia's root issues, but it was an answer to her present dilemma.

Following the initial outpouring of the "Father's Heart" phenomenon, a secondary epiphany occurred with Virginia. This she called the "Heart of the Bride." It was during this time that Virginia truly sensed her purpose, her mantra, her life song—to prepare herself and others, to make ready a pure, spotless Bride for the coming Bridegroom. She studiously searched out the scriptures for any and all insight concerning the Heart of the Bride and desired only to be considered as one of the wise virgins as described in the Gospel of Matthew. Virginia felt a sense of wholeness envelop her. It was revelation and life to her soul. That, too, would be tested and tried in a very real way for Virginia.

The church continued to hold special "Father's Heart" healing meetings for the next several weeks; however, it wasn't long until this precious movement that was insurmountably dear to Virginia's heart became a source of division instead of unity. Human history has a tragic way of repeating itself. There were misunderstandings among the congregation and poor handling by church leadership of this fresh revival. As a result, the church disbanded, and its people scattered only a few months after that profound, holy evening in the church offices. The split broke Virginia's spirit and a new disenchantment began to brew in her heart. It was the catalyst for a soon-to-come rebellious season that would sweep through her life in a fury! And, as was the case with everything else in the life of a highly task-driven, perfectionist-minded, and stubborn woman, Virginia devoted 110% of her efforts to the fall that was to come.

Heartbroken and dismayed, Virginia left the church, wanting nothing to do with its unfortunate demise, yet she couldn't deny the work God began in her. Even though the church split left a bad taste in her mouth, the sweet gift of the Father's Heart and Heart of the Bride encounters would linger with her always. But would it be enough to sustain her through the coming torrent?

CHAPTER 2

The Blues

*I*t was a cloudy Sunday afternoon, and Virginia had a bad case of melancholy. She decided that a walk in Central Park to get some fresh air might lift the doldrums. Normally, she would have been going out to eat with friends after church service, but since the schism, she had little to no fellowship with anyone. "*Maybe this will take my mind off things,*" she thought as she found a little unoccupied spot to sit near Bethesda Fountain and decided to do some people-watching.

Even though it was an overcast and somewhat chilly late fall day, the people were still out and about in numbers. "*Probably getting their last hurrah before the cold snap,*" she supposed as she took her pen and journal out of her bag, ready to jot down thoughts or sketch pictures if so inspired. That journal held a great deal of her creative thoughts, song lyrics, artwork, and the like, but it also contained some very deep-seated, private reflections of emotional conflict, hopes, and dreams. Virginia sat for the next forty-five minutes watching the passersby and creating stories in her mind of their lives—imagining where they worked or what their family life was like. Was theirs a hard-knock life like her folks? Or did they find fortune in a wealthy home with opportunities presented on a silver platter? Were they content? Happy? Or sad and alone as she felt? Her attention was drawn to an elderly gentleman sitting alone on a park bench feeding the birds. His face was particularly spellbinding—not because it was flawless or handsome, but because it had such character and interest in each line and wrinkle. "*He has a story to tell,*" she mused as she began to sketch his face on the paper. Then, below her completed sketch, she began to write...

Across the plaza, you sit in solitude...
outwardly stoic, yet inwardly aflame.
Countless people walk by you every day
but who has ears to hear
the crackling inferno of age...
and who has eyes to see
the veiled secrets of history —
the hidden wants and wishes awaiting.

Somehow... by sovereign design...
this traveler passes by;
my senses awaken as I near you.
I am arrested by all I see.

Forgive me... I can't help but stare.

Your outer walls crumble
as years of loneliness deface you.
Your deep, searching eyes...
Your wrinkled, weathered skin...
Your tough, rugged hands.
But there is so much more to you
beyond these apparent features.

I look at you... deeply... and see
the face of your identity...
Familiar to me — that face.

I feel I know you... as if we've met
As if... (sigh)... who are you?
I long to hear your story
...concealed within mute walls.
To chronicle your lingering memories
that rove in empty spaces.
To give them a resting place
upon paper and within hearts.

I sense your masked passion...
I feel your aged pain...
I'm acquainted with your fears...
and overtaken by your dreams.
But how? I do not know.
I feel I know you... as if we've met
As if... we're one.

Forgive me... I can't help but stare.

A single raindrop fell upon Virginia's journal, and a chilling wind flipped the page. Closing the book, she looked up toward where the elderly man was sitting, but he was no longer there. It began to drizzle a little harder, and Virginia realized she was about to get drenched. Stuffing her journal back into her bag, she was startled by a man's voice.

"It doesn't look like you came prepared today." The man extended his umbrella over Virginia to shelter her from the falling rain.

Virginia looked up and slowly stood to her feet beneath the offered shelter. There he stood, with dirty blonde hair and the most captivating blue eyes she had ever seen, peering over the rim of his glasses. He smiled warmly at her as Virginia stood speechless.

"Hi. I'm Sam. I was just walking by and noticed you sitting in the rain. You're welcome to take my umbrella if you want. I don't have far to go, and I won't melt in a little rain. You, on the other hand…" he chuckled.

Virginia smiled back at him. "That's very kind of you. Very chivalrous, actually. You don't find that much these days."

"Why, thank you," he replied.

"I think I'll just go over to the coffee shop and grab a warm drink. I'll be okay, but thank you."

"Well, let me at least walk you there. It's starting to come down pretty hard now," Sam insisted.

By the time they reached the coffee shop, it was raining cats and dogs! They darted through the doorway, laughing as Virginia exclaimed, "Wow! I'm glad you showed up. I would have gotten completely soaking wet."

"No problem. Glad to be of service." Sam shook his umbrella and sat it in the corner. "You know, a hot drink actually sounds good right now. Mind if I join you, Miss…?" Sam was waiting for Virginia to offer her name.

"Oh, I'm sorry. It's Virginia. But you can call me Ginny. And I don't mind at all. Please, it's my treat. For your kindness, of course," Virginia offered.

"Well then, I'd gladly accept, but my father would never let me hear the end of it if he found out I let a woman foot the bill. I know that's an archaic mindset these days, but even so, drinks are on me." He didn't let her argue the point before making his way to the counter and beginning to order.

There was something about Sam that instantly made Virginia feel at ease. She didn't normally accept invitations from strangers, but she didn't sense any ill intent or danger from him, so "*Why not,*" she thought.

They found an open table in the corner of the shop and sat with their hot beverages. Neither said a word for a minute or two as they were watching the rain pound against the window next to them, sipping from their steaming mugs.

Virginia was the first to break the silence, "So, Sam, do you live in the city?"

"Just outside the city," he answered, "with my wife and two little ones—Willow, who's 5, and Aidan is 3. But I work at a church in the city, Heart and Soul Community Church."

Virginia looked at his left hand and saw the wedding ring. "*Figures*," she thought. "And what do you do there? At the church?" She tried to pull herself together upon realizing the gallant gentleman she just met was already spoken for.

"I'm the worship leader. You know, the music director. I was just headed back there after hanging with a couple of kids from the youth group at the park after church when I ran across you."

"Oh, I'm sorry. I don't want to hold you up, but I appreciate the coffee and the umbrella," she grinned.

"No worries," he said. "I'm not in a hurry. What about you? You live around here?"

"I do. I have an apartment a few blocks from here. And I'm a paralegal at a nearby law firm. Sounds boring, right?"

"Not at all! I'm actually kind of jealous. To be a paralegal, you must have quite an organized and detailed mind. Something I wish I had," Sam joked. Then he posed a more probing question, "So, that's what you *do*. But tell me what energizes you. What's your passion?"

At first, Virginia was taken off guard. It had been a while since someone moved beyond superficial talk to a deeper heart conversation. And she only knew this guy for fifteen minutes. She took a moment to think about his question. "Well, I am good at my job, but I guess what I really love doing is more creative. I love music and writing and…" (looking out the window to the outdoors where, at this point, the rain stopped and the sun was peeking through a cloud) "the beauty of nature. Flowers, in particular. I love flowers."

"That's cool." Sam really seemed interested in what Virginia was sharing. Not like so many self-absorbed people she knew who asked a question out of politeness and then half listened to the answer. He continued, "When I saw you at the park, I think you were writing in a notebook?" His head tilted to the side a little as he was trying to recall the details.

"Yeah. My journal. I saw this elderly gentleman feeding the birds and just felt inspired by him. Probably silly, but it helps me process things… like life," she said with a bit of sarcasm, rolling her eyes.

"I get that," Sam concurred. "Would you mind if I read it? What you wrote today in the park? I'd really love to."

Virginia's cheeks grew warmer as a hint of awkward embarrassment came over her. "I don't usually…" she began.

Sam interrupted her protest. "I don't want to make you feel uncomfortable if you don't want to share it. I would just really love to see your creative work… your view on the world around you."

Virginia hesitated a moment, then took the journal out of her bag, "Okay, why not." Then leafing through the pages, she handed it to Sam. "This is what I wrote today." Virginia felt very insecure and lacked confidence in her creative abilities. She never thought it was *good enough.* Feeling a bit unnerved as Sam began to read, she fiddled with her coffee mug and raised it to her lips to take another sip.

"Wow. Just wow!" Sam exclaimed as his eyes looked up from the pages. "Ginny…" This was the first time she heard Sam speak her name and it gave her heart a jump. "This really is amazing. You truly have a gift. May I?" he asked before thumbing through the other pages.

"Sure," she lowered her head so he couldn't see her blushing.

A few moments passed before Sam asked, "What's this one?" He turned the book towards Virginia and pointed to a song lyric she penned a few months ago, entitled *"Hover Over Us."*

"Oh, that. It's a song I wrote a little bit ago. I haven't done anything with it. It's a long story, but I just came out of an ugly church split and was trying to make sense of it all. So, as I was praying about it, the lyrics came to me."

"I really love it," Sam professed. "Actually, would you mind if I worked on it? There's a community worship and prayer event coming up, and I think it would be perfect. I'd like to hear your take on it. Do you have some time yet today? We could go over to the church and run over some ideas."

Virginia was floored at his interest. She had never given much thought to actually developing the song into something that would be shared with an audience. His enthusiasm lit a dormant fuse in

Virginia. She was both nervous *and* excited about the prospect of collaboration. Before she knew what came over her, she blurted out, "Yes! Let's do it!"

Virginia and Sam spent the next couple of hours sitting at the piano in the church sanctuary, pounding out melodies and harmonies, and working on chord structures and dynamics. To Sam's astonishment, Virginia also had an amazing voice. *"She's full of surprises,"* he marveled as he listened to her sing:

> *Hover over us again...*
> *over the deep*
> *Hover over us again!*

When Sam met Virginia in the park and when they sat in the coffee shop, he obviously noticed her pleasant appearance. But for some reason now, as she stood piano-side, he was smitten by her beauty. Her short, auburn hair framed her delicate-featured face; her deep green almond eyes sparkled in the stage lighting as brilliant gemstones, yet with a hint of sadness within. He noticed when she felt awkward, she would gently bite her lip or push a strand of hair behind her ear. But when she smiled, she smiled with her eyes that lit up the room and his heart. Sam, obviously distracted, hit the wrong chord.

"Oh, sorry! I just lost my place for a minute," Sam quickly recovered. "Look, Ginny, will you sing this at our event? I'll accompany you and sing background vocals, but I don't think anyone else can do it justice."

"I… I'd be honored. I'm a bit rusty, though," she said timidly.

"Please. After what I just heard? I don't think so. It'll be great," Sam encouraged.

They finished working together on the song, sat down on the sanctuary steps at Heart and Soul Community Church, and literally began to share their hearts and souls for hours. They talked about their views on spiritual matters and shared discontent over what had become the mechanics of the institution called "church." They discussed their mutual desire for a return to the church they saw in the Book of Acts and the potential for real, holy, and intimate heaven-on-earth type of relationships in the here and now. Virginia shared what happened with her church split and how much it broke her heart. Sam, likewise, shared his struggles with his dissatisfaction with his present position and his desire to do more out in the community. A more boots-on-the-ground approach, as he called it—wanting to go into bars and clubs with music and connecting people with God on their turf instead of expecting them to grace the doors of a church building. It was a fascinating and invigorating conversation.

Virginia left that day after their conversation on the church steps energized to finally talk with someone who shared similar views, who understood her heart, and who had a passion for the "deeper" things of God. Over the next few months, Virginia started attending Heart and Soul Church, got involved in the worship team, and became close friends with Sam and his wife. She was finally beginning to open up again to a church family. At last, she felt a genuine camaraderie, both creative and spiritual, with someone. But little did she know that this feeling was also taking shape in a much different fashion than she anticipated in Sam, whose Silent Hidden Inner Turmoil was about to hit the fan.

CHAPTER 3

Sam... I Am

Samuel Novak, born in Detroit, Michigan and youngest child of three in the Novak family. (Virginia and Sam had that in common—being the youngest in the line of children.) As a boy, Sam was comical and imaginative. He always had a joke or a tale to tell that entertained the family. Secretly, though, he wanted to be a news broadcaster when he grew up. So, little Sammy would sneak away into a room by himself when he thought no one else was listening, pull out his tape recorder and microphone, and record himself reading the newspaper, a magazine, or even the TV guide on occasion. *"Sam Novak here, coming to you live with breaking news. Fast food chain McDonalds introduces the Happy Meal! Story at 11. Back to you, Walter."* Little did he know that the walls were paper-thin, and everyone could hear his adorable antics.

Life was good as far as Sammy was concerned—bike rides in the summer to the nearby grocer to buy candy with the change he saved in his piggy bank; building snow forts in the winter with his friends and having the biggest snowball fight the block had ever seen; and playing with his best buddy, Max, the loyal Cockapoo (Cocker Spaniel and Poodle mix) who followed him everywhere— but that was all about to change.

At age 9, due to his dad's job transfer, Sam's family moved from Detroit, Michigan, to Garden City, New York. Everything was a new adventure—a new home, a new neighborhood, a new school, and new friends. Unfortunately, there were also new challenges and new threats—a gang of bullies in Sam's block who liked to team up against newbies. And their sights were set on Sam. He was the new kid on the block, and the bully brigade decided to let Sam know who was in charge. For years, they terrorized Sam. It wasn't constant or predictable. That's what made it even harder. One minute, the bullies were nice to him, inviting him to play games with them or ride bikes together. And the next, they turned on him, picking on him, calling him names, and beating him up. Sam had to come up with creative ways to avoid them after school by taking alternate routes home in hopes of throwing them off his scent, as they would often chase him or hide behind trees, waiting to trip him up or kick and punch him. This finally ended one day when the head bully, chief instigator, and leader of the group unexpectedly moved away. Sam heard rumors of the bully's parents and their alleged drug use and trouble with the law, but he didn't know the details of their sudden departure. Quite frankly, Sam didn't really care because, somehow, his absence deflated the dynamics of the bully brigade. Perhaps the other kids just lost interest in Sam and moved on to another helpless victim. In any case, for the first time in a very long time, Sam could walk home from school unscathed. But the damage had already been done to young Sammy. He would have to deal with the repercussions of this trauma for years to come—low self-worth, distrust, isolation, fear, and anxiety.

At age 14, Sam found his first *adult* magazine in a dumpster behind the school. This was the start of a very long uphill battle that developed into an addiction—a way to escape and cope with the emotional pain he experienced on a constant basis. Sam's family was there, but not *really there*. His dad was gone most of the time with work commitments, his mom was emotionally absent and kept herself preoccupied with book clubs and soap operas, and his older siblings were off doing their own thing. Sam was left alone much of the time and didn't feel like he had anyone to confide in or a safe place to land. He felt abandoned, unwanted, unloved, and alone. So, he suffered in silence.

Fast forward. After a few years of military service overseas following high school, Sam returned home to the States and had a few odd jobs here and there. Sam was a very talented and versatile musician by this time, something he cultivated during those difficult teen years. Music kept his head above water, so to speak, when he felt like his world was collapsing in on him. He started attending a local church at the invitation of a friend. It wasn't long before word got out of Sam's musical abilities, and, wouldn't you know it, the church just so happened to need someone to head up the music department. So, Sam, desiring a sense of purpose and belonging, accepted the position of worship leader at Heart and Soul Community Church.

Meanwhile, Sam was in and out of unhealthy relationships for years but, at age 30, finally settled down and married one of the most eligible single women in the church, Hannah. Everyone thought Hannah's conservative demeanor was just what Sam needed to tame his wild, overzealous heart. In terms of music genres, if Hannah was easy-listening, Sam was definitely rock-n-roll. The term "opposites attract" may be true to some extent, but in the case of Sam and Hannah, their polar opposites only amplified after marriage. This polarity, along with the unrealistic expectations each brought to their union, created much unanticipated tension.

One year after they wed, Sam and Hannah had their first child, a baby girl, Willow Novak, followed by a bouncing baby boy, Aidan Novak, two years after that. Sam's children were the light of his world. But as the years went on, the strain of trying to hold everything together and keep up appearances took its toll. Increased responsibilities and involvement with the church became more of a burden than a joy. Those on the outside looking in would say that Sam had it all—a wife, a family, a home, a ministry—yet all the while, his emotions were churning in a vat within him; a gaseous mixture of discontent, anxiety, fear, and longing.

It was over two decades since Sam stumbled across his first pornographic magazine. This sexploitation would fluctuate over the years—for a short season, he would disavow its enticement; and the next, he would go on a binge. His entanglement with pornography tended to escalate during stressful times, and things were getting very stressful in Sam's life.

Sam never really made peace with the trauma of being bullied or the emotional distancing from his parents as a child—the festering wounds oozing to the surface further reinforcing his battered self-esteem. His painful experiences imprinted a certain code of distrust in his psyche, and this distrust in people formed the basis of his addictive behavior as an adult. He could never fully give himself to others—only partially, as being vulnerable with people would mean trusting them not to hurt him or stab him in the back. He lacked a true confidant in life—a support system—those to whom he could completely bare his heart and soul, hurts and fears, secrets and dreams.

Pornography, for Sam, was a way to escape. He could feel connected to something or someone without the fear of that person hurting him, because it wasn't a real relationship. He could escape the fear and anxiety that constantly harassed him by entering a fantasy realm—where here, it didn't matter who he was or what he looked like, what he had, or what he lacked—here, he could feel connected and wanted. It was his only *safe* space. And therein lies the deception. Because it wasn't safe... only an illusion.

Porn taught Sam at an early age that the way to feel fulfilled was to communicate physically, sexually. It took his black hole of deep emotional need, temporarily filled it with the quick fix of excitement and arousal, then left him feeling twice as empty and sucked back into the black hole of despair—like gorging on empty calories from a dozen donuts, only to be hungry again an hour later. And the endless cycle continued, but not only did it continue, it progressed to riskier and more extreme highs—followed by harder and deeper crashes. Such is the monster of addiction. Addiction placed a demand on Sam's body to find fulfillment in any way possible to fill the void and escape the pain, loneliness, rejection, and abandonment. His drug of choice was physical gratification. And it was quickly destroying his relationship with Hannah.

Then... Sam met Virginia. And suddenly, things got even more complicated.

It was like a fresh breeze blew across his soul. They had an instantaneous and profound connection that Sam couldn't shake. For the first time, he felt a connection with someone on a soul-to-soul level, even on a spiritual level. Virginia listened to him. She validated him. Sam felt like he didn't have to perform or live up to expectations when he was around her. He could just simply take off his mask... and... be. Just being near to her filled the black hole—but for how long would that be enough?

CHAPTER 4

The Forbidden

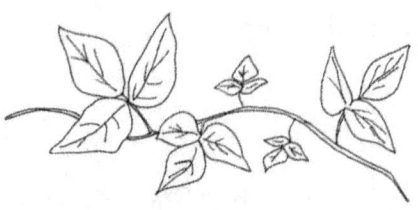

Sam Novak had captured Virginia's affection in unforeseen ways. When they first met, she was not looking for a relationship beyond that of a friendship. In her view, their friendship was still that of sharing common beliefs, hopes and dreams, and mutual disillusions of life. She felt excited to finally meet someone she connected with on such a profound level. But she never took it to the *next* level… until…

That phone call.

Virginia was at work, trying to focus on tedious case files and research, when her phone rang.

"Hi. It's Sam."

"Hi, Sam! How are you?" Virginia cheerfully answered.

"Look, I know you're at work, and I don't really know how to say this…"

Virginia was curious but said nothing.

Sam continued, "But I just can't stop thinking about you. Look, please don't say anything. Just let me finish. I've been feeling this way for months now and don't know what to do about it. Ginny, I'm falling in love with you. I'm sure you don't feel the same way, but I just had to say something."

Silence.

Virginia was completely unaware that Sam was harboring such feelings—and for *her*, of all people! She still wrestled with so much insecurity. Surely, this was a joke. But he wasn't offering the punch line.

Sam spoke up again. "I know I just dropped a bombshell, Ginny. I'm sorry. You don't have to say anything right now, and, actually, I would prefer that you don't. I'm planning to go to the coffee shop by the park this evening. You know, the one where we first met. If you want, I'll be there. If not, I understand. Goodbye, Gin." And with that, Sam hung up the phone.

Virginia sat in disbelief for several minutes. *"What just happened,"* she thought. In a New York minute, her world spun off its axis. Virginia stood up from her desk and began to walk down the hallway, oblivious to her coworkers who greeted her along the way. She darted into the restroom and, with trembling hands, locked the door behind her. Turning on the cold-water faucet, she raised her head to look at her reflection in the mirror. She was somewhat surprised by the look in her eyes staring back at her. Her head was still reeling with confusion, but her eyes were fixed and fiery. She shook her head and splashed a little cold water on her face.

"I'm sure he just needed to vent and confess his inappropriate feelings. He's just feeling guilty," she tried to reassure herself. She was certain his intent was to bring it into the light in order to assuage his guilt. But it backfired. She dried her face and looked once more into the mirror. Somehow, the words he spoke awakened a sleeping giant deep inside of her. Virginia could see it in the fiery green eyes looking back at her. A part of her who had remained silent and dormant for years and years suddenly emerged as Sam's words flipped a switch and activated her.

A knock on the bathroom door jolted Virginia. "Just a minute," she said as she took a deep breath and tried to gather herself before going back to work.

But how could she work now? Her thoughts were erratic and racing; she couldn't concentrate on anything else but that phone call. She removed her reading glasses, held her head in her hands, and rubbed her temples as her supervisor, Shelly, walked by her desk. "Ginny? Are you alright?

"Oh, hi. Sorry. Yeah. Well, actually, no. I'm just not feeling very well at the moment," Virginia muttered.

"Well, you don't look good at all!" Shelly exclaimed. "Why not call it a day? Go home and get some rest, okay?"

"Yeah. I won't argue with you on that point. I think I should go home. Thanks, Shelly." Virginia was relieved as she shut down her computer, grabbed her purse and jacket, and headed out the door.

Upon entering her apartment, Virginia dropped whatever she held in her hands on the floor and collapsed on the sofa. She knew she should forget about Sam's phone call, but for some reason, instead of shunning the notion, Virginia clung to it as if it was the last ounce of water in a drought-ridden land... the last morsel of bread amidst a famine. Danger signs were popping up all around her; alarms were going off inside her head; red flashing lights swirled about her, yet instead of running away from the danger, she found herself wanting to run straight in.

An hour passed of fighting with her inner voice before Virginia sat up and decided to freshen up, change her clothes, and walk to the coffee shop to see Sam. *"I'll just go meet with him and talk this through,"* she reasoned.

Sam was sitting at the same table where they first sat that rainy Sunday afternoon a few months ago. Her heart skipped a beat when she saw him, but she quickly brushed it off and resolutely walked towards him. He stood when he saw her.

"Hi. Uh, wow, you came."

"Hi," Virginia smiled.

Sam grinned at her greeting. Only he knew the significance of her one-syllable, two-letter word—hi. Upon meeting Virginia, a stream of creativity began flowing from Sam, and he was secretly writing songs and poems like never before. He kept it all hidden from Hannah, of course, but he recalled one journal entry wherein he penned:

> *hi*
> *does she feel*
> *all that I feel from such a simple expression?*
> *she should*
> *for there is no way*
> *to contain this eminent force*
> *that seeks passage from my soul to hers*
> *I am a refugee in search of a refuge*
> *she is my shelter*
> *and the entrance to her safety is found in her simple*
> *hi*

"I wasn't sure if you'd show up, so I didn't order anything for you. Can I get you something?" Sam offered.

"No, thanks. Look, Sam, I want to thank you for sharing your heart with me today. I know it wasn't easy for you to call and tell me those things."

"No, it wasn't. I'm sorry if it was inappropriate, but honestly, if I didn't tell you, I felt like I was going to explode."

"I was just kind of floored, you know? I wasn't expecting it, and, well, I didn't know what to say. I really like you, Sam, and I don't want to mess up a good thing." Virginia shifted in her chair, feeling a bit uneasy at the conversation. "You know, maybe I'll grab some water after all."

Without giving her a chance to stand, Sam jumped up, "I'll get it for you. Be right back."

Virginia felt so special and doted on by Sam. It was just his way, and she wasn't used to the attention. She watched as he asked the lady behind the counter for some water, evidently making a funny comment as she laughed and handed him a glass. He always had something witty to say. She loved that about him. Virginia noticed how handsome he looked in his jeans, white t-shirt, and blue blazer. The blue brought out his eyes. *"Stop!"* she thought as she quickly shifted her eyes away.

"Thank you," she said as he sat the water on the table in front of her. "Sam," she continued, "I know things are rocky right now in your marriage, and I just don't think it's a good idea for us to…"

Sam interrupted, "For us to get involved. I know. You're right. So, where do we go from here? I mean, I've sort of let the cat out of the bag with how I feel about you."

"I don't know. And believe me, I'm flattered, and under different circumstances, I wouldn't hesitate. You're an incredible guy, Sam. Any woman would be lucky to capture your affection. But do you think it's possible to continue our friendship?"

"I'm willing to try," Sam replied, but knowing in his heart that he could never be content with mere friendship.

Virginia just smiled and took a sip of water. Who was she kidding? She knew she was crazy about Sam and had no idea how to *not* let it show. But she had to try. After all, he's a married man.

❊ ❊ ❊

Throughout the next few weeks, Virginia and Sam tried to keep things above board and go about a normal friendship. Virginia continued to be part of the church worship team and helped Sam out with administrative tasks that he drastically needed help with. Organizational duties were not his strength. But what he may have lacked in organization and attention to detail, he made up for in spades as far as creativity, ingenuity and vision. At first, Sam and Virginia thought they had a grip on things… fooling even those closest to them. But they both knew they were walking on thin ice.

They had just finished music rehearsal, and the team was gathering up their belongings to leave for the evening when someone asked Virginia, "Hey, Ginny! Are you going on Friday night? Over to Sam and Hannah's house? They're having a surprise birthday bash for Hannah." Virginia looked at Sam, unsure how to respond.

Sam spoke up, "Of course! You're coming, right? I'll need all the help I can get if I'm gonna pull off a surprise party." Sam looked at Ginny and shrugged a little, feeling like what he just said was lame.

"Oh, yeah. Of course. I'll be there. See you all then," Virginia waved as she quickly exited the room. She closed the door behind her, fell back into it, and sighed as she whispered, "I hope this isn't a mistake."

Friday night came before Virginia knew it. She showed up at Sam's house an hour early to help with last-minute preparations. Virginia knocked on the door, and Sam answered.

"Hi. Thank God you're here. I don't think I'd make it through tonight if you didn't show up. You're wearing it," Sam smiled as he took Virginia's coat. He was referring to the chartreuse-green turtleneck sweater she was wearing. It was a Christmas present from Sam and Hannah, that, actually, Sam picked out for her. "You look great."

Virginia blushed, "Thank you," and then quickly walked down the hallway where others were hanging up decorations. "Hi everyone! How can I help?"

The evening went off without a hitch, as far as the surprise element and as far as everyone else was concerned. But if people could see, no, *feel* the sparks that were flying between Virginia and Sam throughout the night, it would have been disastrous. Hannah was lovely, though, greeting friends and family and thanking them for coming.

"Thanks, Ginny," Hannah said as she hugged Virginia. "I heard you played a part in making this all happen. I didn't have a clue," she laughed.

"*No, you really don't,*" Virginia thought as she hugged her back. "I'm glad you're having a good time. You deserve it." And Virginia really meant that. Hannah was a really good person who deserved to be happy, and Virginia hated that she was harboring secret feelings for Sam. "*This is wrong. I should just leave,*" she thought as she turned to walk down the hall to find her coat. Her quest was interrupted as one of the guests grabbed her by the arm and yelled, "Time for cake! Lend me a hand, would you?"

There would be no easy getaway for Virginia, so she decided to take the edge off by hitting the wine bottles in the dining room. One glass turned into two and then three and before she knew it, she was feeling pretty "good"—rather, uninhibited and relaxed. And so was Sam. It's hard to believe no one else noticed their flirtation. The purposeful "Will you hand me that plate?" just so their hands could touch; the walk-by in close quarters just so they could brush against one another; the glances across the room as if no one else was around. Virginia poured another glass of wine, not to take the edge off (as that happened about a glass or two ago), but to ease the guilt she was beginning to feel. It didn't work.

The party was finally winding down and guests were leaving; however, Virginia realized she shouldn't have poured that last glass of wine as she stumbled a bit in the hallway and caught herself along the wall.

"Whoa, Ginny. I don't think it's a good idea for you to drive home. You don't seem too steady on your feet," Hannah came to her rescue.

"You're probably right. I'm so sorry, Hannah. I guess I'm a lightweight when it comes to drinking. I'm not feeling so great, actually," Virginia said as she made her way to the bathroom. A few minutes later, she emerged. Hannah was still standing there.

"That's that. You're spending the night, Ginny. I'll get the bed ready upstairs. You come up when you're ready." Hannah motioned to Sam and quietly said, "Help her up the stairs, okay?" Then, she proceeded up the staircase to get the spare room ready for Virginia's unplanned stay.

Sam came alongside Virginia to steady her in the hallway. His arm wrapped around her waist as she leaned into him. Then, raising her head, her eyes meeting his, she said, "I'm so sorry, Sam."

"It's okay, Gin. Just take it slow. Lean on me, and I'll help you upstairs to bed." Then step by very slow step, Sam helped Virginia upstairs.

For Virginia, the next few hours were spent either worshipping the porcelain god or tossing about in bed, wishing the room would stop spinning. But as odd as the situation was, Sam never left her side. He told Hannah, since she had an early morning appointment the next day, to get some rest, and he'd watch over Virginia for a little while. And that he did—helping her to and from the bathroom, wiping her face with a cool washcloth, and even softly playing his guitar at her bedside to try to comfort her. If the whole situation weren't so far over the line, it would be heart-warming. Hence, the seeds of the "Forbidden" fully took root, and so began the affair.

At the outset of the Forbidden, as with any new relationship or infatuation, there was a sense of excitement. Illicit desires spawned flames of passion and engulfed the soul as breathless anticipation fueled each encounter with a firestorm of emotion. Each encounter was driven by that force of desire like a tumbleweed propelled by the force of the wind. Momentary phone calls just to hear one another on the other end of the line. Poems and songs penned in a sleepless night. It all became fuel to an ever-consuming fire within. But it was never truly satisfied, so there had to be another encounter. And another. And another. Until it became like a drug that Sam and Virginia could not live without. The quick fix of a rendezvous was fleeting, and they were constantly preoccupied with thoughts racing through their minds, devising plans to connect again at any cost. It became an obsession, really. A flame addiction.

When the emotional connection wasn't enough, they inevitably crossed the flesh barrier. As a result of the patterned fallacies that were imprinted in Sam's psyche throughout his life and years of porn use, the only way he knew to communicate his feelings for Virginia was physically. And Virginia felt the only way she could please Sam and keep him "coming back" to her—to keep him from leaving—was to respond in kind. Their emotional needs underpinned their sexual needs.

But because both Sam and Virginia were followers of Christ, conviction seized them on a daily basis. When they weren't wrestling with God over their choices and sinful lifestyle, they shut down in self-preservation mode, licking their wounds and becoming numb—just trying to survive. In addition to carrying the weight of infidelity, Virginia and Sam were both battling their own personal demons. Sam was war-weary from years of pouring out from an empty cup as a worship leader of a large demanding church; the victim of childhood bullying and emotional neglect; struggling with a long-term pornography addiction; and his inability to connect with Hannah, resulting in a failing marriage. Virginia was fighting a life of low self-esteem and a sense of inadequacy, striving for perfection because of her fear of failure, and recently disenchanted by church relationships. Because they were both imploding to various degrees as individuals, they found common sanctuary in one another.

In total, the affair lasted for almost four years—off and on. Heart and Soul Community Church handled the ordeal to the best of its ability, although, in Virginia's opinion, the church had a long way to go in learning how to rescue and restore its own people. Sam was asked to leave his position at the church, and Virginia was summoned to a private meeting with some *well-intending* church leadership in an attempt to talk some sense into her and cast demons of lust out of her. Virginia, existing in a fog and feeling like a mere shell of a woman to begin with, walked away from that meeting further disenfranchised by the church and filled with anger that people were casting things out of her that simply were not there... all the while neglecting the things that were there—shame, confusion, and hurt. So, shortly thereafter, Sam and Virginia turned their backs altogether on church and God.

It's a crazy thing, though, God's relentless love. Even though they turned away from God's ways, He continued to pursue them—leaving the ninety-nine sheep on the mountain in search of the one (or two in this case) that were lost—wooing them to return to their First Love. While Virginia tried hard to ignore it, she could sense the Holy Spirit drawing her amidst the darkness. One minute, she would be encouraging Sam to go back to his wife, buy her flowers, and try to make it work... and the next minute, she was missing him and holding tight as to never let him go. And Sam, desiring to be with the woman who completed him, yet missing his children and wanting to be there for them, was tormented constantly. It was a continual pinball match of the soul.

One afternoon, as Virginia sat alone in her apartment, just having depleted her reservoir of tears once more, she looked over at the bookshelf across the room. There sat her Bible, untouched for the most part since the onset of the Forbidden. Feeling a certain inner compulsion, she grabbed the Bible from the shelf and laid it on the table in front of her. Having absolutely no direction where to turn, she haphazardly opened it to a random page and began to skim the text. Then, as if leaping from the pages into her spirit, she read from Jeremiah, chapter 17, verse 9:

> *The heart is deceitful above all things,*
> *And it is extremely sick;*
> *Who can understand it fully*
> *And know its secret motives?*

Virginia knew in an instant the truth that confronted her at that moment. All along, she had been listening to what her heart desired. She was listening to its wants and urges—its secret motives. But as a result of listening to her own heart and emotions, she was caught in the clutches of deception which was making her very sick, indeed.

CHAPTER 5

Grace-Bearer

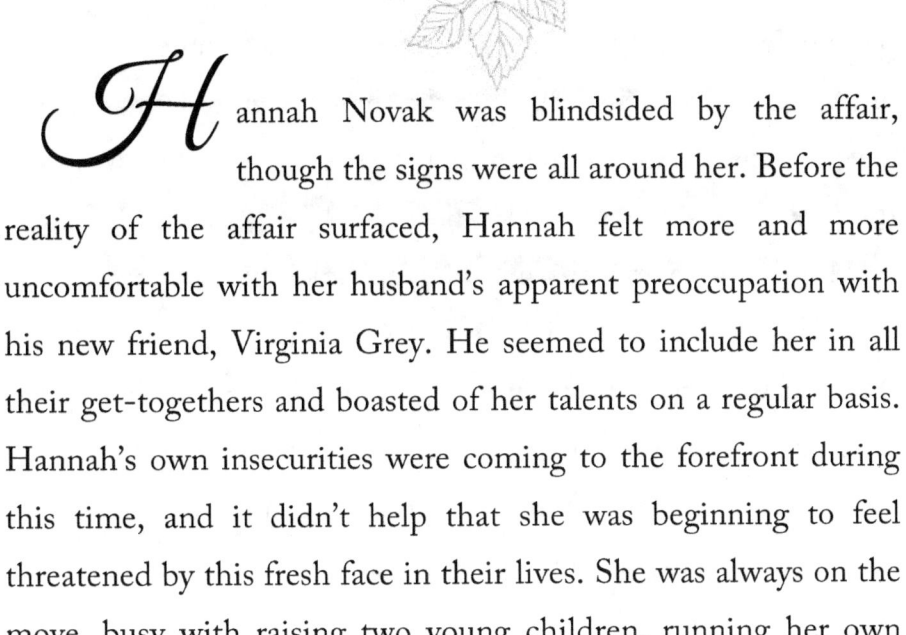

Hannah Novak was blindsided by the affair, though the signs were all around her. Before the reality of the affair surfaced, Hannah felt more and more uncomfortable with her husband's apparent preoccupation with his new friend, Virginia Grey. He seemed to include her in all their get-togethers and boasted of her talents on a regular basis. Hannah's own insecurities were coming to the forefront during this time, and it didn't help that she was beginning to feel threatened by this fresh face in their lives. She was always on the move, busy with raising two young children, running her own massage therapy business, involvement with the church and, now, trying to keep her marriage from falling apart.

At first, meeting Sam Novak seemed like kismet. He was the perfect man for her ideal storybook romance. A successful worship leader at the time who was well-liked by everyone. A creative, spirited soul who shook her out of normalcy. The reformed "bad boy" who brought adventure to her life. And everyone in the church agreed they were a match made in heaven. So, what could go wrong, right? Apparently, a lot.

While Hannah was uncomfortable with Sam and Virginia's friendship, she still believed her marriage would survive this temporary bump in the road. Perhaps Sam's fondness for Virginia was just a novelty... she was new and interesting and needed a place to heal from her former church split. Maybe once that wore off, Virginia would just drift into the shadows, and Hannah would have the full attention of her husband once more. But that was not the case.

Months upon months of trying to hold things together and hoping for the best, Hannah could no longer deny the obvious. All signs were pointing to full-blown infidelity. So, gathering the courage to confront Sam, she posed the difficult question, "Are you having an affair with Virginia?" A question she never imagined she would utter in her lifetime. The answer shattered her into a million pieces. "Yes."

The ensuing years for Hannah were fraught with much sorrow and heartache over the deep betrayal she experienced. The indescribable pain, sadness, and hatred towards Sam and, especially, Virginia, as the other woman, surmounted all other emotions. Yet, in her heart, she still held out hope that restoration could be attained. She wanted to believe that the God who brought Sam into her life to begin with was able to bring him back home again. And so, through tearful prayers, she kept the door of hope open for a time.

There were momentary indications that gave rise to that hope, as both Sam and Virginia attempted to do "the right thing" and sever their bond so Sam could return to his wife and children. But somehow, their attachment drew them back together again. This tug of war went on for years until, finally, Sam and Hannah made their separation final and a divorce was decreed.

One year after the divorce, Sam and Virginia got married. Hannah recalled how difficult that day was for her, as both Willow and Aidan, ages 10 and 8, respectively, were in the wedding. They were so excited to be part of the big day. Willow and Aidan loved their new stepmom and always came home with stories of the fun weekend adventures they had with Daddy and Ginny. While Hannah was happy that they had such a good relationship with their Dad and his new wife, in the face of a "broken home," she was also disheartened at the loss she felt and the difficult challenges this new dynamic posed. Things would definitely never be the same.

The road to healing and forgiveness was a long and arduous road for Hannah to traverse. The rejection and betrayal cut deeply into her very soul, and for the sake of her own wellness, a choice was to be made—the choice to hold onto bitterness or to forgive. Through her years of counseling and her deep Christian faith,

Hannah knew the higher road to take, but would that mean letting Sam and Virginia "off the hook" for their actions? She wasn't sure she could do that. She wasn't sure she *wanted* to do that.

But God, in his mysterious ways that are much higher than mankind's ways, had a plan and a purpose amidst the ashes of brokenness. He desired Hannah's freedom from the cruelty unduly thrust upon her. He desired redemption for all involved. Hannah had to decide whether to continue to rehearse the wrongs done to her and hold Sam and Virginia in contempt or release them into God's care and His justice. So, day after day, month after month, year after year, she chose to walk in forgiveness. She continued to pray for God to help her connect with her choice to forgive, as her emotions had not yet caught up to the decision. But within each choosing, Hannah felt a fresh wave of resolve and relief wash over her.

Hannah, having just finished going over homework assignments with the kids and sending them off to bed for the night, cleaned up the dinner dishes in the sink, then curled up on her oversized chair and pulled her favorite throw over her legs. All day long, she felt a stirring in her, but she didn't know why. She only knew that she needed to quiet her soul at that moment, be still, and listen. Hannah was filled with thankfulness as she sat in the stillness. She was so grateful for all the Lord brought her through over the years—for the friends and family who stood by her and supported her, for divine protection and provision over the years, for the healing she received as sweet myrrh applied to her soul, and for so very much more. As she sat and reflected on the many blessings in her life, Virginia's face came to the forefront of her mind. This shook Hannah from her state of tranquility and caused a tinge of uneasiness in her gut.

"OK, Lord. What's that all about?" she whispered. "Why are You bringing up her again? I've forgiven her… many times." At this point, it was almost three years since Hannah and Sam's divorce and his subsequent marriage to Virginia. Hannah was beginning to rebuild her life, move on, and even date again. So, why was she thinking about *her* again?

Hannah rose from the chair and went to the kitchen to make a cup of herbal tea, hoping it would calm her. Still feeling a stirring within her, she returned to the chair and sat once more in the presence of the Lord. Again, thoughts of Virginia surfaced. Hannah sat her cup of tea on the side table and saw her notebook. Compelled to pick it up, she inquired once more, "Lord, what are you trying to tell me? I've released Ginny to you, haven't I?"

Immediately, she sensed the Spirit's reply, "Have you *really* forgiven her? Then make it known."

Hannah was reminded of the meaning of her name—Grace and Favor. She believed God had equipped her with a divine means of help and strength to walk in grace and to extend grace in her circumstances. She literally felt its power, enabling her to be a Grace Bearer. And now, she was given an opportunity to bestow that gift to another—Virginia.

She knew what was required of her. The Lord was asking to take her to a new level of forgiveness. Up to this point, Hannah had never really received an official apology from Virginia. She wanted to hear the words "I'm sorry," but would hearing that really make a difference? So, out of obedience, Hannah picked up the pen, opened her notebook, and began to write:

Dear Ginny,

As I was praying tonight, the Lord placed you upon my heart. We both know that the past few years have been difficult, to say the least. And while I have struggled with resentment towards you over all that has transpired, I want you to know, Ginny, that I choose to forgive you. I no longer hold onto the offense. But I release you to the Father's care. I truly sense the love and affirmation that God has for you, and I hope you sense it as well. Praying for His many blessings upon your life.

Most sincerely, with love,
Hannah.

Hannah placed the notebook back on the table and took a deep breath. Peace filled her heart, and she sensed the Lord's quiet voice saying, "Thank you."

❀ ❀ ❀

Virginia got home from a long day at work and began sifting through the mail for anything important when she noticed an envelope addressed to her attention. She mindlessly opened it, skimmed to the bottom of the letter, and read, "Most sincerely, with love, Hannah." Virginia practically fainted as her knees buckled under her. She sat down and read the most powerful and clearly prayerful words ever written to her.

It was as if a dam burst forth in the heavens. Hannah's letter opened up the gates of reconciliation between the betrayed and the betrayer. This opened the door for Virginia to do something she wanted to do for a very long time but didn't know how or when the right timing would be. The next day, Virginia called Hannah to humbly acknowledge the hurt she caused (especially to Hannah and the kids), confess her wrongdoing and ask for forgiveness. God's hand was truly at work redeeming the wayward child. Not only did Hannah's brave and selfless act of forgiveness free her from the angst of the fight, but it also extended the power of grace for Virginia to be restored to the Father's Heart. The Road to Redemption was being plowed before them through Fields of Forgiveness.

CHAPTER 6

Believe It Or Knot

*V*irginia closed her eyes, swallowed hard and took a deep breath to calm her present state of anxiety. Never before had she felt so vulnerable as she did at this very moment—Lying face up on a table in the dimly lit room, her naked body covered only by a bed sheet, and the very strong and capable hands of the woman she and her husband betrayed tightly gripping her neck.

Hannah was a certified massage therapist and extremely good at what she did. Virginia definitely needed help. For years, she suffered from chronic headaches and neck pain, and she was desperate to find some relief by any means possible. But never in a million years did she think it would be at the hands of *this particular* woman—the ex-wife of her husband, Sam Novak. The woman who she and Sam betrayed by their affair. Hannah was in a very unique position that day. She could easily get her retribution by strangling the very life out of the "other woman" with her bare hands as she lay helpless on the table. How easy it would have been for Hannah to exact her revenge for the years of pain and sorrow caused by Virginia and Sam's actions. But as awkward as the situation was, Virginia remained on the massage table and put her trust in the woman she once hurt to use her hands for healing instead of vengeance.

"Are you comfortable? Warm enough?" Hannah asked as she rubbed her hands together in preparation for applying the lavender-scented essential oil to Virginia's neck and shoulders.

"Yes, thank you. It's perfect," Virginia replied.

And, indeed, it was perfect in that little room (apart from the dynamics of their unconventional association). The aromatic scents of lavender, chamomile, and cedarwood filled Virginia with comfort as she inhaled deeply once more. And the peaceful, relaxing instrumental music playing in the background quieted her soul. Normally, and under different circumstances, Virginia would have politely asked the massage therapist if he or she minded that they did not converse so she could just get lost in the quiet and enjoy the massage. But in this instance, the silence felt unnerving.

"Thank you for seeing me today. I know you have a busy schedule," Virginia broke into conversation.

"Of course. I was surprised to get Sam's phone call, but I'm glad he reached out."

Sam had a way of breaking down barriers, whether it was comfortable or not! He tended toward the rip-off-the-Band-Aid approach. When he first told Virginia that he had contacted Hannah about scheduling a massage for her, Virginia was taken aback. By this time, Sam and Virginia had been married for three years, seven years from the start of all the madness. And while she recognized they all had come a long way in reconciling differences, this was another level entirely! Her initial reaction was to say no and tell Sam to call Hanah back to cancel. But at Sam's insistence that Hannah really was the best massage therapist he had ever known, Virginia agreed to keep the appointment. After all, she was desperate for relief.

Hannah continued, "You certainly do have some big knots in your neck! Let me focus here for a while, okay?"

"Yes, please!" exclaimed Virginia. "I think that's why I'm having such terrible headaches. No one else can seem to work it out."

And work it out, she did. Hannah really did have the strongest, most therapeutic hands Virginia had ever experienced in a massage. Even though she felt pain as Hannah pressed each trigger point, it was the healing kind and didn't last long as her muscles began to relax.

"I know this is a bit awkward for both of us, Hannah. And I have to admit that for years, I've been all knotted up inside over everything that happened and the people who were hurt, maybe not intentionally, but it's all the same. So, it's no wonder that my neck is so tight from the stress. I just can't let things go." Virginia started to tear up a little and fought to hold it back.

"Oh, Ginny. I've released you from all that long ago and have chosen to forgive you and Sam. God's done an incredible work of healing in my life, and I no longer hold that over you," Hannah reassured. "Don't think we'd be here if I did," she joked.

"I know. Thank you. Your letter meant so much." Virginia recalled the day she opened the letter that released the flood of pent-up emotions and unspoken words to pour out from its reserve.

Virginia's thoughts were interrupted as Hannah applied deeper pressure to the tightened muscles in her neck, referring pain to the front of her head. *"Ow! Was that on purpose?"* Virginia thought as she flinched a bit. *"Guess I deserve it."*

"I'm sorry, Ginny. Is that too much pressure?" Hannah softly asked.

"No, no. It's fine. You just found the problem spot, and it's a bit tender, that's all."

Hannah finished her massage and excused herself from the room to give Virginia privacy. "I'll just be outside when you're dressed. I'll get some water for you. Take your time." As Virginia rose from the table, she shook her head, dumbfounded at the most bizarre yet rewarding hour she ever spent. *"What in the world! I don't know what to do with this, God,"* she thought as she got dressed and opened the door.

Hannah was standing at the front desk with a glass of water in hand. "Here. This will help your body flush out any toxins that may have been released during the massage."

"Thank you," Virginia replied. "Really, I mean it. Thank you for everything."

"Look, Ginny, I don't know how, but God has done something special here. I can truly say that I desire the best for you. There was a time that if I had my hands around your neck like just now, only one of us would have walked out of that room alive." She chuckled, as did Virginia. "But I want both of us to move forward from here. Forgiven and free. And I think it's just the beginning. I feel God's redemption story—our redemption story—will be used to help other women someday. We'll just take it a day at a time and see where it leads. But Ginny, you've obviously been holding a lot of stress in your body. You need to be able to release all the shame. I'll be praying for you."

The two, once in opposition, now embraced in amity.

CHAPTER 7

Ten years passed since the dawn of the Forbidden and things began to settle into a normal routine of sorts, at least on the surface. Virginia and Sam were building their marriage despite the chaotic and unorthodox beginning. They bought a little fixer-upper outside of the city that needed a little TLC, but they were up for the challenge.

Sam, having been dismissed from his leadership position at the church, embarked upon a new career path of working with people with physical and mental disabilities, particularly using music therapy as a means of helping them. Upon completing his education, which he started years before but had never finished due to *other distractions*, he began a substitute teacher position in the school district's special education department. He was finally finding his niche.

Virginia continued her work as a paralegal, but most of her free time was spent as a caregiver for Mama Grey, who became very ill the prior year. Daddy Grey was dealing with his own physical ailments and was not capable of caregiving, so Virginia and her siblings undertook the responsibility of caring for their mother, which Virginia did gladly. Her desire to honor Mama Grey during this difficult time far outweighed any inconvenience it may have posed.

With each passing year, making peace with the past became a little easier, as time tended to be the great mender. But it didn't mean that there weren't consequences to face or issues to still rectify within Virginia. She was angry, albeit discreetly, with the choices that she made and the people who were hurt as a result of the affair—even resentful with Sam over things that happened in the thick of it all. That anger and resentment seeped out occasionally through her passive-aggressive behaviors. If it were up to Virginia, she would have rather forgotten the whole thing happened to begin with. But that wasn't really an option, given the fact that there were children in the mix.

One of the things that Virginia respected the most about how Sam and Hannah handled their separation was that they never spoke ill of one another or even about Virginia in front of the children. They continued to encourage their respective parental roles in the midst of hardship, preferring one another for the sake of peace, and it showed in the children's lives. Transitions were not a stressful occurrence but rather something the children looked forward to.

Even amidst the best possible scenario in terms of sharing custody, being a stepmom was still a challenge for Virginia. She saw the bond that Sam had with his children, but it wasn't the same for her. She adored her stepchildren and loved spending time with them, for they were truly a joy and, despite the challenges they faced from a broken home, were very well-adjusted and happy children. While Virginia was not their biological mother, she was honored to be their "bonus" mom, but this held a mixed bucket of emotions that she tried hard not to show. On one hand, she had these beautiful children that she loved to care for while in her keeping. And on the other hand, she lacked the innate bond that a biological mother possessed.

As the kids grew older and were involved with various school activities—such as band concerts, children's choir, dance productions, and plays—Sam, Virginia, and Hannah all attended every time. They didn't want to miss any of these adorable moments. But Virginia would often feel like a third wheel as she sat among crowds of parents, eagerly awaiting their little one to grace the stage. As she sat there, feeling disconnected at the moment, she would watch the faces of parents as they, ecstatic with pride, watched their little boy or girl as if they were the only one(s) on the stage. Their connection was so intense. It seemed as though they were experiencing something on a much greater level than she could ever know, for she did not have that same bond. Virginia wondered if she would ever have that maternal feeling.

After years of trying to conceive but unable to get pregnant, she finally went to the doctor. The results confirmed her fear. It was medically improbable that she would ever be able to conceive a child. This was yet another huge blow—a deep ache that echoed in the void of her heart. She thought, perhaps, this was some judgment on her life as a result of her season of waywardness—the Forbidden. Perhaps there was a link between her barrenness with her prior sexual sin. Shame agreed with this line of reasoning. It must have been punishment.

The years continued to march on. The children were making plans of their own for the future; Hannah got remarried to her knight in shining armor, Lucas Maddigan, who rescued her from the Tower of Travail she occupied for so long; and Mama Grey...

Mama Grey was ready to be free of the chains of sickness and disease and shed her mortal shell in order to embrace eternal life. Virginia spent every possible minute at her mother's side in those last days—caring for her, praying for her, singing over her, holding her, comforting her, and reassuring her that death was not to be feared and paled in comparison to what Mama Grey was about to experience. These were the most indescribably heart-wrenching yet precious and rewarding days of Virginia's entire life. Little did she know that she would be walking the same road with Daddy Grey as he was reunited with Mama several months later. This season of grief was very deep. Their relationship was so instrumental in Virginia's life, and it was hard to grasp the reality that they were no longer just a phone call away. But she was grateful that they were no longer suffering and were completely healed and experiencing the wonders of heaven. Never did she imagine that her parents' passing would be so double-edged—bitter *and* sweet.

Another year passed with haste. The day, Mother's Day. The weather reflected Virginia's mood—gloomy and overcast, with the threat of rain in the forecast. She didn't mind but actually found it consoling. The cheerfulness of the sun would have only driven a knife deeper into her heart today. The kids were spending the day with their *actual* mom, and Virginia was grieving her inability to have children of her own. Plus, this was the first Mother's Day without Mama Grey. She missed her terribly. Sam was upstairs starting to paint one of the bedrooms, so Virginia decided to join him.

"Hi, sweetie. How's it going?" She could tell by the smudges of paint on his clothes and splatters on his face that perhaps the paint had the upper hand.

"Hey, Gin. Well, I think I have more paint on me than on the walls, but it's going. Do you like the color?"

"I do. It's calming." Virginia smiled at him.

But Sam could see that she had been crying. He knew why. "Come here," he said as he laid the paintbrush down and motioned to her.

Virginia didn't even care that the misty gray-green paint was getting on her, too. She buried her face in Sam's chest and cried once more. "It all just hurts so much."

Sam held Virginia for a few minutes, then, upon wiping her tears, lightened the mood by teasing, "Well, now that you're all messy, you might as well grab that roller and help."

And help, she did. Before long, the room was all painted and pretty as could be. They sat on the floor to admire their work. There was something else bothering Virginia, aside from the Mother's Day woes, but she didn't quite know how to broach the subject. "*I guess there's no easy way about it*," she thought, then dove straight in.

"Sam, can I ask you a question? It's kind of out of the blue."

"Of course. Shoot."

"Well, it's about your past history with pornography," she timidly expressed. "I know you basically experienced a miracle as far as being set free from your addiction."

And a miracle it was! Sam recalled that holy moment as he shook his head in acknowledgment. His struggle with porn and sex addiction was intense and ongoing. But one day, after a deed of the impure kind, the Lord spoke to Sam. "*I have an amazing life ahead of you, but you cannot bring this with you any longer.*"

The Lord's admonition was gracious and frightening at the same time. Sam felt like it was a day of reckoning. He had a choice to make—death or life. Sensing the gravity of the ultimatum, Sam immediately repented by turning away from pornography and choosing obedience to honor God in spirit, soul *and body*. His life was changed as the Lord delivered Sam from the desire to engage in porn from that day forward. In an instant, his 30-year prison sentence was commuted. It was truly a miracle!

But in the days and years that followed God's sovereign intervention, Sam was diligent in working out his sobriety, battling against the urges and neurological pathways etched in his brain. He knew he didn't want to go back to that world again. If he wanted to lay hold of the promise of God set before him, he knew he *couldn't* go back. So, he gathered a few close friends that he knew were also struggling with the same issue and met with them on a regular basis for accountability. At the time, Sam didn't recognize his struggles as an addiction. No one was openly talking about it in that vernacular in his circles. But upon researching the matter closer, Sam discovered that there were organizations that dealt with that very thing—porn and sex addiction. He then learned that he couldn't fight an addiction with the same tools that one fights a struggle. He had to dive deeper, gain understanding, and acquire the tools necessary for long-lasting recovery. So, Sam, re-grounded in God with restored hope, focused his ever-waking thoughts on walking in this new-found freedom.

Virginia continued to share what was weighing heavily on her heart, "Well, I guess what I want to know is…" She paused.

"Go on," Sam insisted.

"Were you still watching porn when we were together? I mean, after we got married? We never really talked about it. I guess I shouldn't have waited eight years to ask," Virginia smirked.

Sam's eyes turned downward as he scratched his chin, formulating his response. He looked back up at Virginia, who had a look of worry in her eyes. "Yes," he admitted. "For the first few years of our marriage, I was still watching it."

Virginia tried not to overreact. But suddenly, things were beginning to make sense. She could never pinpoint it, but now that Sam admitted the truth, it all added up.

"I'm so sorry, Ginny. I never meant to hurt you, too."

Virginia took a deep breath. "I know. It's just that I felt like something wasn't right, but I didn't know what or why. I thought maybe it was me because of how our relationship started, you know?"

She proceeded to explain how, especially during that time period, she felt an uneasiness inside. When they were intimate, she felt dirty and objectified. In the throes of it all, she would find herself praying, "Please, God. Let this be pure in your sight." Then, often, after they made love, she would close herself in the bathroom and cry. But none of it made sense. After all, they repented of the affair and had received forgiveness from God and from the betrayed spouse. Yet she still felt unclean and soiled, like their intimate moments were defiled. But it all made sense now. She was being used as an object for his twisted sexual fantasies. *"How could I have been so stupid,"* Virginia thought.

They both sat quietly for a few minutes. Neither spoke a word, as Virginia's thoughts were racing, unsure of how to react to it all. Finally, Sam broke the silence. "Are you okay?"

Again, Virginia inhaled a long, deep breath and then slowly exhaled. "Yeah. Well, not really. But I will be. I just need some time to process how I feel about it all."

"I understand," Sam reassured. "Ginny, I am so very sorry. I hate it. I absolutely hate what it did to me... to us. But please know that is all in the past, and I never want to make you feel that way again."

Sam extended his hand to her, and hesitating for a few seconds, Virginia placed her hand in his. It would take some time for her to come to grips with his disclosure. The emotion began to overflow once more as she placed her head on his shoulder and wept. Just then, Virginia's phone alerted that a new text message had arrived. She unlocked her phone and read the text sent from the kids, "Happy Mother's Day, Ginny. We love you!"

❀ ❀ ❀

The following day was met with sunny skies and brighter moods. Sam rose early in the morning and surprised Virginia with bagels and coffee. They both had the day off work and, in favor of taking a mental health day, chose not to do any work on the house or stress themselves out over paying bills or doing chores. They decided to take a walk since the weather made a turnabout.

"I'm so glad it's a nice day. The last thing I would have wanted was to be stuck inside because of the weather on our day off," Virginia stated.

"Agreed," Sam said as he took Virginia's hand and began to stroll down the sidewalk. "We could go to Central Park if you want and hit up that coffee shop later."

"Nah. That's okay. This is perfect." Virginia surprised herself at her gut reaction. The truth was there were too many triggers in that section of town. Too many reminders of the days of the Forbidden. And actually, the more she thought of it, the more she realized that New York held way too many painful memories. Things she tried hard to ignore for the sake of moving on. Everywhere she turned, there were so many triggers.

"You're quiet," Sam commented. "Penny for your thoughts."

Virginia grinned, "You'd be a rich man."

"That many, huh!" Sam laughed.

"Just too many to make sense of right now. You know…"

"A woman's brain," Sam completed the sentence. "I know." They both had a good laugh as they rounded the corner of the block. Then Sam got a little more serious. "I got a call this morning."

"Oh, yeah? From who?" Virginia inquired.

"My cousin, Mick. The one who lives in Tennessee."

"Right. And how is Sir Michael these days?" Virginia said amusingly. She met Sam's cousin a few years ago and recalled his fascination with the Knights of the Round Table. His office was filled with knight statues and figurines, medieval pictures and swords, and a bookshelf full of legendary stories. So, Sir Michael seemed fitting.

"You're the only one that can get away with calling him that," Sam laughed. "But he's doing fine. He called to let me know about a possible opening in the Special Education Department in their school district."

"In Tennessee?" Virginia sounded surprised.

"Yeah. Guess he just thought of me. I don't know. It's probably crazy and too far away, but it sounded interesting."

Virginia thought for a moment before speaking. "Actually, Sam, it doesn't sound crazy to me at all."

Sam stopped walking and looked inquisitively at Virginia. "Really? You would entertain the possibility of moving?"

"More than you know," Virginia replied. "I've been thinking a lot lately about our lives here in New York. I feel like there are too many ghosts here, Sam. Do you know what I mean?"

"I think so, Gin. Wow. I didn't think you'd go for it."

"Well, my only question is, what about the kids? We stayed in this area for them so you could co-parent and be involved in their lives. Would you be okay with moving so far away now?"

"I know that will be the hardest thing for me. But Willow's off to college, and Aidan isn't too far behind. I feel like they are at an age now where they're more independent and forging their own paths in life. I definitely want to talk to them about it, but I think it could work."

"We'll make it work. We could fly them down throughout the year, and we'd come back up to visit on occasion," Virginia added.

"So, should I call Mick back? Should I get more information on the job then?" asked Sam.

"Yes, I think so. Absolutely. Why not!?" Virginia felt the dark clouds that were hanging over her for so long begin to disperse. Maybe this was the answer. Maybe now was the time for the meaning of her married name, Novak, to become a reality—New. Perhaps now was the season of new beginnings for Virginia and Sam.

CHAPTER 8

Dream a Little Dream

Wearied by the visitation of yet another sleepless night, Virginia groped in the darkness for her phone on the nightstand next to the bed. Heaven forbid she ever lose that phone. She had come to depend on it for everything. An address book, a photo album, a calendar, a notepad for shopping lists, or random thoughts that she didn't want to slip her mind—but most important to her right now—a clock!

Her hands fumbled about the nightstand for a few seconds, accidentally knocking over a tube of ChapStick® that rolled across the stand to the base of the lamp. Finally, her fingers lay hold of the device. Rubbing her tired eyes, she squinted to read the illuminated time. 2:22 a.m. Funny. Those numbers again. If she weren't so annoyed by the fact that she was still awake at such an ungodly hour, she would laugh at the irony. But she was too tired to be humored. With the exception of a few boxes stacked in the corner of the spare bedroom, Virginia and Sam were finally all settled into their new house in Tennessee. Virginia was not one to take a long time to unpack. So, upon their move, she jumped straight into nesting mode and couldn't rest until everything was in its place.

2:22… Virginia rubbed her eyes again. She was always intrigued by how often she would see these repeating numbers when she looked at the clock. Clutching the phone next to her chest, her mind drifted as she recalled when the significance of these recurring numbers first began—2:22, 11:11, 4:44. Virginia recalled the quick messages, emails, and phone calls she and Sam would make and receive whenever one of those times was seen. It was a secret code of sorts meant to carry a message of pining and infatuation. A designated point in time when two people, separated by distance and circumstance, could still share the sentimentality of a single moment, like looking at the moon at the same exact time from different locations and whispering a name like vapor into the night air, as if the moonbeams could carry a message of love across the miles. She shook off the crazy romanticism.

How strange and fanciful it all seemed to her now. Virginia's eyes grew heavier as she allowed her head to sink deeply into the soft pillow, oscillating between wakefulness and slumber… ever so slowly drifting… deeper… and deeper into sleep… until…

❅ ❅ ❅

Wild, colorful imaginations of secret codes and private messages spanning over time and space as rainbows through the sky; swirls of words and whimsical poems, penned on butterfly-embossed scrolls, taking flight and fluttering past her mind's eye; imagery of childhood games and visions of innocent little girls playing hand-in-hand on the freshly cut lawn...

"Ring around the rosy"

... the scent of lavender blooming in the garden and the early morning sun shining on bright pink and yellow-flowered dresses...

"Pocket full of posies"

... the warm summer breeze blowing ribbon-tied ponytails in the air like kite tails in the sky...

"Ashes, ashes"

... darkening skies ominous with pending gales and storms. Flashes of lightning. Gusts of wind. Booming thunder scattering tiny feet, running for safety and screaming...

"We all fall DOWN!!"

Virginia jolted out of her dream at the sensation of falling, dropping the phone she still held in her hands. Her sluggish reflexes were unable to catch the phone as it slid off her satin sheets and plummeted to the hardwood floor. Thud!

She quickly looked over to Sam lying fast asleep next to her, unaffected by the commotion. She took a moment to come to her senses, retrieved her phone from the floor, and plugged it into its charger before carefully returning it to the nightstand.

With her heart still racing from the startle, she breathed a deep sigh before settling back into the warm bed. She looked once more over to her husband and whispered, "2:22, I love you," then rolled onto her side and pulled the covers tightly around her in hopes of a swift and more peaceful slumber.

The smell of freshly brewed coffee awakened Virginia's senses.

"Good morning, sleepy Gin. You sleep okay last night?"

Removing her eye mask and rubbing her light-sensitive eyes, Virginia responded with a tone of concern, "I guess so. Why do you ask?" She had hoped that Sam didn't notice her restlessness in the wee hours.

"No reason. You just didn't budge at all when I got out of bed this morning. Seems like you were dead to the world!"

Funny he should use that phrase, she thought, because that's exactly how she felt. Dead to the world. It had been years since she felt truly alive inside. She thought for sure the move would reinvigorate her and fill her with a newness of purpose and zest for life. Not that she was entirely *unhappy* with her life. She loved Sam, of course, and knew he adored her. His tireless acts of service and constant gestures of devotion reassured her of that very fact. But the ravages of former transgressions and their consequences took a toll over the years. Even after all this time, she still felt a perpetual numbness, as if a sliver of her soul had been deadened. Now that most of the tasks of unpacking were behind her, maybe she could just settle in and enjoy life.

"Want some coffee?" Sam asked as he poured a fresh cup.

"I do, but I'll get it in a minute," she swung her legs around and sat on the edge of the bed. "You're up early for a Saturday."

"Yeah," Sam nodded his head. "I had some ideas swirling in my head as soon as I woke up. You know, about the winter outreach program. Thought I better commit them to paper before they slipped away."

Sam took on his new role at Hopeland School District's Special Education Department seriously, and he was excited to be given the responsibility of heading up their annual outreach program. His background as a musician would come in handy this year, as they were taking on an original musical. The focus of this year's outreach was the senior center in the nearby village, which he embraced wholeheartedly. He found great joy in bridging the gap between people groups and generations.

From the very instant they moved to Hopeland, Tennessee, Sam dove head first into his work. The phone call from his cousin, Mick, informing him of the open position earlier that year was truly a God-send. Virginia felt like she was suffocating amidst the chaos of the big city life and was desperate to move... anywhere, really. She just wanted out. And Hopeland was the perfect breath of fresh air that they both needed.

"By the way, did I tell you that I'm having lunch with Mick today? He sent me a text late last night, and I couldn't remember if I told you."

Virginia, still trying to get her bearings upon waking up, replied, "Umm, no, I don't think you mentioned it, but that's fine. I have to meet with the realtor today, anyhow. She's going to show me a shop at the edge of town that just went on the market a few days ago."

"That's great, Ginny. I'm really proud of you for taking this step. You know that I believe in you, right?"

Sam bent over to kiss her on the forehead as she was still sitting on the edge of the bed, his hand holding a cup of coffee also tipping with his body as he leaned closer. "Whoa! Watch it!" Her hands steadied the mug, keeping the coffee from spilling over the rim. "Yes, sweetie, I do know that." She pressed her forehead into his tender kiss. "Thank you."

"Okay. Since you obviously don't want to wear my coffee," he snickered, "I'll let you get up and make your own cup. I'm headed downstairs to work on the computer for a bit."

At that, he grabbed his notebook and glasses off the nightstand and moseyed down the steps. Virginia could have sworn she heard him humming a Christmas tune as he went. "*It's only October,*" she thought as she shook her head and chuckled.

Grateful that Sam gave in to her request to put the coffee bar in the bedroom sitting area for mornings like this, Virginia made her favorite honey latte, sprinkled it with cinnamon, and sat in her Granny's wingback chair to gaze out the window of the quaint nook. It was a perfect fall morning. The sun was just breaking through the canopy of oak trees, revealing the deep wine-crimson leaves of the dogwoods at the edge of the yard. The autumn colors were just beginning to emerge in all their glory. It was her favorite time of year. She loved the crisp chill in the air that gave rise to cozy blankets and oversized sweatshirts.

Despite the charming song of the warbler sitting momentarily on the window ledge before flying over to the nearby birch tree, Virginia was haunted by another tune. "Ring around the rosy..." The imagery from her dream began to make its way to the forefront of her mind. *"What an odd dream,"* she thought. She could recall the images and colors in great detail now.

This made her think about Daddy Grey's sister, Maybelle. Aunt Belle lived in Manhattan until her passing several years ago. She was a tad eccentric... okay, maybe more than a tad. She was quite a sensational woman who livened up every family gathering with her singing, dancing, and storytelling. She would often speak of mystical phenomena, holistic remedies, supernatural encounters, and the like. But she especially loved the topic of dream interpretation. *"I wonder what Aunt Belle would say about this one. She'd be analyzing every detail, I'm sure."* Details like little pony-tailed girls playing childhood games, the scent of lavender, and flashes of lightning from an approaching storm.

Trying to push it away from her mind, she drew the quilted throw over her lap and took another sip of coffee when a sudden movement outside the window caught her eye. A mischievous, determined little squirrel was trying to outwit the squirrel-resistant bird feeder that hung from a branch of the birch tree. He tried and tried but kept slipping off. "*Funny but determined little guy*," she thought. But the silly antics of the squirrel didn't hold Virginia's attention for long before her dream reemerged... "Ashes, ashes..." That line was particularly troubling, as it now conjured emotions of scared little girls running for safety from the impending storm. And then there was the falling...

Her intense thoughts were interrupted by the cell phone ringing on her nightstand. "Who would be calling me on a Saturday morning," she mumbled as she made her way over to the bedside. The caller ID read Margaret Holland. The realtor she was to meet today.

"Hello?"

"Hi, Ginny? It's Maggie... Maggie Holland."

"Yes, Maggie. How are you? Is everything still on for today?"

"Yes, but that's why I'm calling. I may have to push our meeting back a couple of hours. Can you meet later today, say around 2:00?"

"Of course. That's fine. My schedule is flexible today, so I'll meet you at 2:00."

"Thanks so much. See you then!"

Virginia was actually grateful for the extra time she was just allotted. This would give her a chance to take a walk through the nearby park and clear her head. Ever since the move to Hopeland, she'd been too preoccupied with unpacking and nesting and hadn't much time to simply explore the neighborhood, so this was the perfect opportunity. She just couldn't shake the tinge of anxiety she was feeling from her restless night, and that strange dream, so maybe a brisk walk would help. As she placed the phone back on the stand, the words sliced through her consciousness... "We all fall DOWN!"

CHAPTER 9

A Little "Berti" Told Me

It was truly the perfect fall day. The crispness of the air and the warm rays of the sun were in perfect harmony. The occasional crunching of the fallen Ash leaves underfoot was a delight to the ear. One of the reasons Fall was Virginia's favorite time of year was the introduction of boot season! She must have had a dozen different kinds of boots in her closet that had all made their way to the front row of the shoe rack. Today, she wore the most comfortable walking boots she had as she strolled down the cobblestone path towards the park. She made sure to leave the house in plenty of time to enjoy some downtime before making her way to the edge of town to meet Maggie.

The park was lively, with dog owners throwing balls or Frisbees for their fury, four-footed friends to chase. Moms and dads seizing a few minutes outdoors for their energetic tots to run off some steam. And people like her who just needed an enjoyable place to meditate or read a book. After walking around the pond once, watching the light ripple across the water and dodging the haphazard cast of a little boy's fishing rod, Virginia decided to rest on a nearby park bench. Not seeing a vacant bench anywhere, she chose the one situated under the magnolia tree closest to the pond. She shared the bench with what appeared to be an older woman in her mid-80s, perhaps of Central European descent, she thought. The elderly woman, wearing a mustard color hand-knit sweater and flowered bucket hat, was reading a book, the title of which Virginia couldn't quite make out. No matter. She wasn't interested in striking up conversation anyhow. She just wanted to rest for a while and enjoy the warmth of the sun before continuing to her appointment.

It couldn't have been more than thirty seconds before she heard a somewhat feeble but sweet voice break through her barrier of thoughts.

"Beautiful day, isn't it?"

Virginia turned to the elderly woman next to her, who, at this point, placed her book on the bench between them. She recognized the author of the book. Beverly Lewis. Virginia grinned slightly as she recalled Mama Grey's love for Beverly Lewis' Amish fiction novels. Sometimes, her mom would open a new book in the morning and finish it by evening. Virginia was always amazed at how fast she could read a book. This recollection evoked a sense of warmth, which Virginia accepted with gladness.

"Yes. It really is," she responded, her attention quickly turning from the woman to a sweet little girl attempting her first steps in the cool, leaf-covered grass... barely clinging to mom's fingers as she tumbled to her knees, giggling.

"I don't believe I've seen you in the park before. I'm here almost every day, weather permitting, of course. But sometimes I get so caught up in my books that I don't get to people-watching, so I might have just missed you."

Virginia turned her eyes back to the elderly woman who was eagerly awaiting a reply. "Oh. Umm, no. I don't get to the park as often as I would like. My husband and I moved here not too long ago, and I just haven't been able to explore the area much yet." Virginia's attention once more diverted to the little barefooted girl who was now climbing on the back of a Goldendoodle like it was her personal little pony. The longsuffering puppy tolerated it for a little while, then simply laid down and rolled over on his side as if to say, "All done."

"My name is Berti." She extended her delicate, weathered hand and waited for the distracted woman sharing her bench to acknowledge the gesture.

Virginia, now embarrassed at her apparent lack of manners, reciprocated by extending her own hand to Berti's. "I'm so sorry. I didn't mean to be rude. It's so nice to meet you, Berti. My name is Virginia."

"Virginia. What a beautiful old-fashioned name."

"Thank you. It was my grandmother's name. Most people call me Ginny, so you're welcome to call me that if you'd like, Miss Berti."

Berti smiled from ear to ear, but her beautiful hazel eyes smiled even brighter. "Then Ginny, it is." Berti glanced over at the little girl that had been drawing Virginia's attention. "Do you have children of your own?"

A cloud of sadness settled upon Virginia like a morning fog covering the cold waters of a lake. The question shot emotions as shards of glass throughout her body. She had always dreamed of having a little girl of her own someday and then, perhaps, a little brother to follow. But those dreams were shattered upon her last visit to the doctor. While she tried to accept her condition, her heart was still raw at the mention of the topic of motherhood. Trying not to let Berti see the profound sadness that had just gripped her heart, Virginia swallowed hard and simply said, "No, I don't."

Berti was an extremely perceptive woman, and despite Virginia's thinly veiled attempt to conceal the sadness, she saw right through it. Years of experience, a life lived hard yet gracefully—one of trials and sorrows, of joys and tranquility—instilled much wisdom and compassion in this aged woman. Realizing the gravity of the question she had just asked and Ginny's terse response, Berti tenderly replied, "Nor do I, my dear."

Glancing over to the playful, tumbling little girl, Berti added, "At least none of my own."

Both women looked at one another with an unspoken understanding, and Berti's compassionate smile put Virginia at ease. *"At least none of my own?"* Virginia thought that was an interesting choice of words and knew there must be more to it, but she didn't want to pry. After just a few minutes together, she felt a genuine connection with this beautiful old soul—as if she'd known her all her life. The two allowed a few moments of stillness to overtake them before Virginia broke the silence.

"Miss Berti, it certainly was a pleasure sharing a bench with you today. But I'm afraid I must be on my way if I'm to be on time for my appointment."

"Of course, my dear. The pleasure was mine as well. Have a wonderful day. And, Ginny, remember, I'm here almost every day if you ever care to join me again. Until the weather gets too cold, of course. Then I have a little table over at the café across the street that practically has my name on it," she winked.

"That would be lovely," Virginia impulsively responded. She surprised herself with her quick response because it wasn't usually her way to be so eager to connect with people she didn't know. But she really did mean it. She hoped to spend time with Berti again very soon.

It was just a short walk from the park to the edge of town, where Virginia was to meet the realtor. She made it with ten minutes to spare, so she found a shaded bench across the street from the shop to rest and gather her thoughts for a few minutes. Surveying the area around her, she began to allow herself to envision the corner flower shop she had always dreamed of opening.

This spot was exactly what Virginia had hoped for. The perfect corner lot at the end of the cobblestone road. It was both a quaint and convenient location. She could practically see the outdoor displays of seasonal varieties with their splashes of color against the gray brick wall. A fresh coat of white paint around the Victorian trim work would be all it needed to freshen up the exterior. Maybe add a couple of ornamental corbels around the large picture window. That would surely make it pop. Last but not least, a handcrafted sign above the door that would read "Peace Rose Boutique" in honor of Mama Grey's favorite flower. After all, her mom was the true inspiration for this venture to begin with.

Virginia recalled the many afternoons spent pulling weeds and pruning rose bushes in the flower garden with Mama Grey in her wide-brimmed hat and garden gloves, straightening the little metal and wooden sign that so proudly displayed "Nana's Garden." Virginia loved that garden, not because of the flowers but because of the joy it brought to her mom.

Before Virginia had the chance to fully envision in her mind's eye the crimson pink and cream drapery that would frame the storefront window to embody the colors of the peace rose, she was jerked into reality as Maggie called her name from across the street.

"Ginny! Hey, Ginny! Yoohoo… over here!"

Maggie Holland was a force to be reckoned with. Outgoing and confident, it's no wonder she was the most recommended and top-selling realtor in the region. Her golden blonde hair and bright blue eyes precisely reflected the spark of her carefree personality. Over the past couple of weeks of searching for the perfect location for the flower shop, Maggie had become a good friend. And Virginia had few of those since moving to Hopeland. Given last night's disquieting dream and Virginia's melancholic start to the day, she welcomed Maggie's upbeat disposition.

Maggie greeted Virginia with her usual European-style kiss, sweeping from right to left cheek. "I believe this could be the one, Ginny!" Maggie exclaimed. "I can't wait to show you the inside!"

"And I can't wait to see it. The outside is perfect, Maggie. It's as if you can see straight into my mind and know exactly what I want."

"Well, it has been said that I possess certain psychic tendencies." Maggie laughed her contagious laugh while fumbling through the keys to open the shop door.

They walked inside, and Virginia took a deep breath. Despite the worn, soiled carpet, chipping paint, and fallen ceiling tiles, she could see the beautiful potential. She saw straight past the imperfections and visualized the shabby chic décor, complete with a corner tea table and water feature wall. Her head was spinning with possibilities.

"Well? What do you think?" Maggie interrupted Virginia's stream of thoughts.

"It's perfect. Absolutely perfect!"

"I thought so, too. I had hoped you would feel the same. The building has been in the same family for over 75 years. For the right person, I know the seller will move down on the price a little."

"Why are they selling now?"

"Well, the family has come into some rough times and health issues, and they just are not able to handle the upkeep any longer. It's been empty for a while, and they would rather it be given fresh life than waste away to nothing."

"I can do that—give it fresh life."

"I don't doubt that for a minute, Ginny. Tell you what, if you agree, I'll contact the seller and give them your offer. Let's meet up in a couple of days to go over the details. Okay?"

"Sounds good. Maggie, do you mind if I take just a couple of minutes longer to look around?"

"Oh, take your time! I have a couple of phone calls to make anyhow, so I'll be outside." At that, Maggie made a dramatic about-face and scurried through the door like a woman on a mission.

Virginia noticed a small wooden chair in the corner of the room. She made her way over to it and sat down, allowing herself to dream a little more of the shop's potential. *"This would be the perfect spot for a little round table to sit and enjoy a cup of tea,"* she imagined. Once more, she couldn't help but think of Mama Grey. Oh, how she loved her tea. And Virginia loved those moments when they sat and talked while sipping a hot cup of her favorite Red Rose tea. "I wish you were here to see this, Mama," Virginia whispered. Tears began to well up in her eyes. "This is my new start. You always told me there was a brighter future ahead of me. I can't quite see it yet, but maybe this is it. I have to believe that this is it." She wiped her tear-streaked face as she stood to her feet. "I miss you, Mama. But this will be our special place. A place of peace. The Peace Rose."

By the time Virginia composed herself and walked outside, Maggie was finishing up her phone call.

"Looks like some storm clouds are moving in pretty quickly. Did you walk here, Ginny? You want a ride back home?"

"No, I'll be fine. Thank you, though. I'll just walk fast and try to beat the rain."

"All right then. Be careful. I'll call you as soon as I have an answer from the seller."

Maggie gave Virginia a quick hug and hopped in her bright yellow VW. Virginia chuckled and waved goodbye as Maggie drove away, seeing her little blonde-haired ponytail bop to the music pumping through the speakers. As Maggie drove off, Virginia could hear her singing background vocals to some song playing on her radio as loud as could be... "whoa! yeah, yeah!"

It was only about a 15-minute walk from the shop for sale on the outskirts of town to Virginia's house. If she hoofed it, she'd hopefully beat the rain.

As Virginia briskly walked along, her mind kept returning to the possibilities of the shop. It really was the perfect location and she could envision every detail so vividly. As each corner of the finished room became clearer and clearer, she found herself brimming with hope. A feeling she hadn't felt in a long, long time. In fact, it scared her. Virginia wanted so much to embrace this new venture with excitement, but something kept her from believing that she deserved it, not after everything she'd done.

"I shouldn't get my hopes up," she thought. *"Probably just another pipe dream."* She shook her head as if to shake the thoughts of optimism from her brain.

The storm clouds were moving in faster than Virginia expected. A gust of wind whipped through the street as she walked past the corner deli shop and practically took her breath away. She picked up the pace to a jog. But before she knew it, the storm was upon her. The clouds suddenly released a deluge of raindrops that fell to the ground in a fury. Virginia began to sprint to find shelter and escape the storm, but a bolt of lightning in the sky stopped her in her tracks. She stood there in the middle of the road in the pouring rain. Paralyzed.

CHAPTER 10

'Flashback' of Forbidden Fruits

With her head tilted upwards and eyes tightly closed, the rain washed over Virginia, drenching her from head to toe. Her entire body felt frozen as she stood motionless amidst the storm in the middle of the road. She was no longer aware of her surroundings as suppressed memories began to surface and demand her undivided attention. The emotional undertow carried her far away, as if teleported through a flashback, to a place she thought she securely locked up and left behind—the Forbidden.

❀❀❀

The hum of the bathroom fan filled the otherwise quiet room of Virginia's small apartment. She clung to the shower wall for support as she tilted her head upwards. The warm water cascaded over Virginia's face, mixing with the tears that bitterly flowed. If only she could be washed away from this life and its sorrow. If only she could go back and make different choices. How did she get here!? "Please make it end," she whimpered as she dropped to her knees and then curled into a fetal-like position on the shower floor, sobbing uncontrollably for what seemed like hours. Somehow, the warm water upon her skin comforted her, albeit momentarily. If only this water could cleanse her on the inside, too. If only it were that easy. As she lay there motionless, she watched as the water flowed down the drain, wishing it could carry her pain away with it.

Virginia mustered the strength to rise to her feet again, shut off the shower, and reached for her towel. Every movement seemed so labored. Simple tasks took twice the effort, and her body felt like she was 200 pounds overweight. On the contrary, Virginia's skinny frame had lost weight over the last several months. If she were to be honest with herself, she'd realize she was borderline anorexic, starving herself of even basic sustenance. Partly because she just had no appetite. But partly because she was punishing herself. After all, she didn't deserve to be satisfied and happy.

The phone rang in the other room of Virginia's small studio apartment, forcing her to shake out of her self-contempt. She started towards the phone but stopped halfway, deciding to let the answering machine take the call. ...please leave a message after the beep...

"Hi Ginny? It's Mom. I must have just missed you. I just wanted to see if you are planning to come to the picnic this

Saturday afternoon. Give me a call then, and we can talk about what food to make. Okay? Love you." Click.

Virginia sighed a deep breath and then threw herself into the corner chair. Social gatherings sucked the life out of her, especially now. She had become quite good at disguising what she was going through… wearing masks of smiles and laughter, all the while feeling numb inside. Making sure to say all the right things and manipulate conversations in order to avoid others' probing questions and curiosity that may unwittingly reveal the truth that she was so carefully hiding.

She couldn't keep avoiding her mother's calls, and there were only so many times she could use work as an excuse to get out of family gatherings. She decided to plan her getaway in advance so that she wouldn't have to stay long. She didn't know how much longer she could wear this façade, but it helped that she had two young nephews. She could just safely play with them and keep them entertained for most of the afternoon. They never prodded her with meddlesome questions or got too personal. After all, the topic of conversation never got deeper than skinned knees from a bike smashup or superhero stories. They were the perfect escape. She decided she'd take them on a scavenger hunt during the picnic on Saturday. That would keep her otherwise engaged.

Virginia looked at the clock and realized how late it was getting. She'd never make the bus to get to work in time at this rate. But she forced herself to get up nonetheless. Making her way to the bedroom, Virginia stood at the closet riffling through her clothes for something to wear until finally, her arms fell to her side as she blankly stared at the hanging wall of fabric.

"I just can't do it today," she muttered to herself as she made her way over to the phone again to dial her work number. "I'll just take another sick day."

Virginia lay curled up on the sofa most of the day, periodically turning on the TV to try to keep her mind from obsessive thoughts. But the events of the previous night kept seeping to the forefront. Restless, she sat up and grabbed the long-sleeve denim shirt lying across the sofa arm. She clutched it to her chest before burying her face in it and taking a deep breath. The combination of warm, spicy mahogany and a slight fruity scent from Sam's cologne still lingered in the material. She loved that smell. Oh, how she wished she could hold the man she loved instead of clinging to a shirt with his lingering scent.

Virginia lit a candle that was placed in the middle of the coffee table and sat for what seemed to be hours, just staring at its dancing flame. Its movement fascinated her. She longed for the flame of passion that was ignited in her heart to be able to dance freely. Instead, it felt like it was being smothered.

Virginia felt a slight twinge of hunger as she sat there, her emotions numb but mesmerized by the candle. "*Maybe I will make some toast, at least,*" she thought, hoping it would somehow ease the gnawing she felt in her gut. It was the oddest juxtaposition of normality and madness as Virginia tried to go about a daily routine. She buttered a piece of toast and placed it on the countertop in the kitchen, recalling his kiss on her neck as she stood in that very spot the night before. She shook her head to try to clear her thoughts as she walked to the sofa and collapsed again. It wasn't long before Virginia's thoughts drifted to the bittersweet events of the previous night.

At twilight, there came a knock at her door. And suddenly, her heart skipped a beat. She knew it could only be one person. Sam. She practically ran to the door, breathless... with each step seemingly higher off the ground than the last. "*Why does this man have this effect on me?*" she thought. She didn't give herself enough time to answer that question before opening the door for her lover.

No words were spoken. Nothing needed to be uttered at that moment. Just the embrace. Virginia threw herself into Sam's chest and let him hold her until the chill of the evening air forced them to move inside. Sam handed her a present—a small, beautifully ornate box. Inside was a red rosebud and a piece of paper rolled up like a scroll. She opened the paper and read:

SHE USHERS IN SPRING . . .

She ushers in Spring
And hers is the scent of love that all the world perceives
While the blossoms bloom and the leaves awake

from their wintry slumber
While oceans warm and fresh rains feed
the creatures of the wild
She will be my sun, my longing, my reason
for greeting the morning
She ushers in Spring
And in the wake of her arrival, it wafts of sweet
perfume and romance... and kids at play.

These words were the most beautiful she had ever read. Tears filled her eyes as feelings of loving and being loved, desiring and being desired, acceptance and being accepted overwhelmed her. Sam and Virginia talked for hours, held one another, and shut the rest of the world out. At first, it seemed like a scene straight out of a romantic movie. She wanted the storyline to continue forever, but harsh reality hit as the imaginary director yelled, "CUT!"

No. Not yet! Please, can't this last just a little while longer? But Sam had to leave and sneak *back home* unnoticed, with any luck, before sunrise. Virginia was unaware of what excuse he may have used to be out so late on a weeknight, to begin with, but she was certain it was convincing. At least it had been up to this point.

After the door closed behind Sam, Virginia turned to see his light blue denim shirt left behind. She didn't dare take it to him. Instead, she picked it up and held it close to her as tears began to flow bitterly. It's all she had of him until the next brief encounter. The sadness began to eat away at any remaining bliss that accompanied the forbidden visit. Now came the regret, the ache, the shame.

Virginia lay on the cold floor with Sam's shirt as a pillow under her head, trying to hold tightly to the memories of the preceding hours before they completely slipped away. She tried desperately to relive the scenes of this love story over and over in her mind, but it always ended too soon. The rhythmic sound of an old movie projector reaching the end of the reel grew louder and louder in her head. If only she could make it through this day. Perhaps tomorrow would bring another chance rendezvous. She had to hope for that, or her world would crumble.

Virginia gently shook herself out of daydreaming as the sun began to stream through the window and beat against her skin. Normally, she would welcome the warmth. But this morning, it felt intrusive... too cheerful. After all, her misery desired company. So, she arose from the sofa to close the drapery and allow the darkness to befriend her.

Virginia picked up the plate of a half-eaten piece of toast, went to the kitchen, and threw it in the sink. Maybe if she laid down for a little bit, she would feel better. After all, she barely got a wink last night. As she proceeded towards her bedroom, Virginia caught a glimpse of herself in the hallway mirror. She stopped for a moment and looked at the person staring back at her. She hardly recognized herself. A dwindling figure with loose clothes hanging from her frail frame. Puffy eyes from hours of crying darkened to reflect her soul's condition. She then whispered, "How did I get here?" And with that, a sense of loathing overwhelmed her as she threw herself into bed.

"We all fall DOWN!"

$\mathcal{A}$nother bolt of lightning struck up the road ahead of Virginia, bringing her back from her momentary flashback.

"Ginny! Ginny, dear! Get yourself in here. Hurry! You'll catch your death of pneumonia out there!"

Virginia looked in the direction of the voice and saw Miss Berti standing at the door of a café across the street. Regaining lucidness, Virginia ran over to the café out of the storm.

"Oh, my dear, you're absolutely soaking wet! What were you doing just standing out there like that? What were you thinking!?" Miss Berti said as she handed Virginia a tea towel that the petite, brunette waitress, Lois, intuitively tossed across the counter to them.

Embarrassed at her apparent stupor a few moments ago, Virginia tried to dry herself off and sat at the nearby table... her hands still trembling.

"I don't know, Miss Berti. I'm so sorry. I must look a fright!"

"Oh, my child. Don't you worry. You're as pretty as ever. However, your eyes tell a different story. They're as stormy as the weather out there. Are you okay, Ginny?" Berti's voice became serious with deep, warm overtones. She motioned Lois over to the table and ordered some tea.

"You do drink tea, don't you?" Berti asked.

"Yes, I do. Although, I prefer coffee in the mornings. But a cup of tea sounds perfect right now." Ginny smiled with gratitude.

"Duly noted, my dear. Now, back to my question. Are you okay?"

Virginia looked down at her still trembling hands and began to fiddle with her rings as she tended to do when uncomfortable and avoidant. Normally, she would have provided a sugar-coated response accompanied by a well-rehearsed and masked smile. But for some reason, she felt at home with this tender soul across the table. "I think I'm okay now," she said.

"Here you go, sweetheart," Lois said as she placed a steaming teapot with a delicate pattern of trailing ivy leaves and matching cups on the table. Next to it, she placed an assortment of herbal teas and fresh English biscuits. "Berti, honey, you just let me know if there's anything else you need, okay?"

"Thank you, Lois. This will do for now," replied Berti.

The smell was delightful to Virginia's senses. She took a moment to take in her surroundings after so hastily rushing into the café to find shelter from the torrential rain still pounding on the bay window. The café was small and quaint with a mash-up of design elements including Eastern European knick-knacks, old-fashioned doilies, and English tea sets, alongside modern sculptures and canvases of minimalist paintings. It was an eclectic mix, but the overall ambiance of the café could best be described as grandma's kitchen with a modern kick. Virginia would later discover the reason for the fusion of décor was that the owner's daughter was studying art abroad. The splashes of modern artwork throughout the room were undoubtedly her creations, proudly displayed amidst the traditional backdrop. The sign hanging over the door read, "The Cinnamon Shack."

Virginia poured herself a cup of tea and took a biscuit from the tray. "These biscuits are delicious. And this tea is hitting the spot," she said with a sigh of relief. "Thank you."

Berti's eyes looked up from her steeping teabag. They lit up the room as she smiled.

Virginia continued, "Miss Berti, I hardly know you. I mean, we just met this morning at the park and yet I feel like you know me. Somehow, your eyes see right through me. And the funny thing is, I'm okay with that. I feel safe with you. That must sound crazy."

"No, not at all," Berti reassured. "I'm glad you feel that way, dear. Sometimes, God brings people into our lives for very special times. I felt that today as we were sitting on the park bench together. Go on, my child. Tell me what's troubling you."

"I don't even know how to put it into words." Taking a sip of tea, Virginia allowed its warmth to calm her before proceeding. "Have you ever felt like there was something following you? I don't mean a stalker or anything like that. I mean, something more profound. Like a sort of imaginary monster looming in the shadows. You can never really see it, but you know it's there. Just waiting to pounce at any given moment."

Virginia looked at Berti's face, expecting to see an expression of shock. Instead, she was met with the most compassionate and inviting eyes. Berti didn't speak a word but just nodded in understanding.

"I just feel haunted by some things, I guess. Things from my past."

"I could tell something was wrong. I couldn't believe it when I looked out the window to see you standing in the pouring rain."

Virginia held her face in embarrassment, "I feel so silly now."

"No, no, no. There's no need to be embarrassed. You're okay now. You say you feel haunted by something. What do you mean by that?"

Virginia proceeded to tell Berti about the strange dream she had the night before and that haunting children's rhyme that she kept hearing over and over in her mind. Yet she dared not divulge the details of her recent flashback that caused her to stand frozen in the middle of the street in driving rain. She felt comfortable around Berti, but the shame of her seedy past prevented her from divulging the details.

"Now, that's an interesting dream, Ginny. I think dreams are a gift. When the language of the soul is at a loss for words, it can speak through a dream. There must be something special about this dream. Some deeper meaning for it to linger with you all day like this. Don't you think?"

Virginia was fascinated by Berti. There was obviously much more to her than met the eye. Virginia thought for a minute about Berti's profound statements before responding, "I guess there must be a reason. But I hadn't thought about it being a gift. It was so disturbing that it felt more like a nightmare. So, you're saying maybe there's something my subconscious is trying to tell me?"

"Or God," Berti quickly replied. "Maybe when you get home, you should pull out a notebook and write it down. Then you can pray about it. Ask Abba to show you what it means."

"Abba," Virginia repeated. She was familiar with the Aramaic name used for God the Father found in scripture, similar to how a child would use Papa or Daddy. Hearing Berti say Abba reminded Virginia of the Father's Heart movement years ago. It brought a great deal of comfort to her upon hearing Berti use this expression of intimacy and respect for the Father, for she hadn't heard many people use it so naturally. It seemed second nature to Berti.

"You know Him then," Berti said with a smile. "I'm so pleased!"

"Yes, I do. I've had a lot of ups and downs in my spiritual journey, but I do. That's so beautiful, Miss Berti. And you're right. I think it's a great idea to write it down." Virginia lightly chuckled. "You remind me of my Aunt Belle. Funny, I was just thinking about her this morning. She loved dream interpretation. She passed away, but I sure wish I could talk to her about all this. She'd love it."

"I'm sorry to hear that. She sounds like she was very special to you. Maybe you could take a page out of her playbook and give it a shot? Dream interpretation, that is," Berti smiled.

Virginia looked at the cuckoo clock hanging on the wall. It was just minutes away from emerging and performing its little song and dance to greet the new hour. "Oh my! It's almost 5:00 already. Where has time gone? I should be on my way. Thank you so much, Miss Berti, for coming to my rescue today. I've really enjoyed our time together. Please let me take care of the tea and biscuits," Virginia pulled out her wallet.

"The pleasure was all mine, Ginny. And no need for that," she said as she gently pushed the wallet back towards Virginia. I come here so much I have a tab. They take good care of me here. We could make a weekly date of it if you want?"

"Actually, I would love that," Virginia gladly responded. "Friday afternoons are usually good for me. Would that work for you? Maybe around 1:00?"

"Perfect," Berti replied. "I look forward to it."

"Me too. And maybe they'll start a tab for me, too," Virginia said amusingly as she gave Berti a hug. "See you next week!" she exclaimed as she waved a friendly goodbye to Lois and opened the door to leave.

Thankfully, the storm passed, and a ray of sunshine broke through the clouds as Virginia began to walk home. The air was fresh with that after-rain scent. Deep and earthly. She took a deep, drawn-out breath. The day certainly hadn't played out as she anticipated, but in that moment, she felt a sense of peace. Something she hadn't felt in a long time. She reflected on the day's events—the park, the flower shop, the café—and then she felt a nudging within her as thoughts of the dream and the flashback resurfaced. She knew something was stirring in her soul that would require her to pay attention and no longer ignore it. She knew she had been pushing her emotions down for way too long, even to the point that it was physically affecting her with persistent headaches and digestive problems. Perhaps now she would be ready to face her Forbidden past and be released from the chains that bound her to its torment. She recalled what Berti said in the café...*dreams are a gift. There must be something special about this dream. Ask Abba to show you...*

It was around 5:20 p.m. when Virginia reached the house after her roller-coaster day. Her emotions were raw, and she just wanted to go straight upstairs and collapse in bed. When she opened the front door, though, Sam was already in the kitchen prepping for dinner.

"Hey! There you are! I was starting to wonder whether or not I should send out the cavalry to find you," Sam laughed at his archaic reference.

"Cute," Virginia replied, barely able to muster a slight giggle. She made her way over to Sam and kissed him on the cheek.

"Wow, you look like you've been through the wringer. Is everything okay? How was your appointment with the realtor?"

For a moment, Virginia forgot what her appearance was after being caught in the rainstorm a couple of hours prior. "Oh!" She exclaimed. "Yeah, I'm fine. I was walking back from the shop and underestimated how fast the storm was moving in. Got soaking wet. But an interesting story."

Virginia proceeded to describe her afternoon. Walking to the nearby park and meeting Berti, then haphazardly running into her again at the café where she ran for shelter. Sam remained attentive as she shared the events of her day while chopping fresh tomatoes for dinner. He was particularly pleased to hear how much she loved the building for sale and its potential for the flower shop.

Sam was always so supportive of her endeavors. Her greatest fan, he always said. And Virginia appreciated his undying encouragement. They'd been through a lot together, and this fresh start in a new town felt imbued with hope for a change. Virginia certainly prayed this was the case.

"Enough about me," Virginia blurted out as she grabbed the boiling pot of spaghetti noodles from the stove. "Tell me about your day. How's the program planning going? Oh, and you had lunch with Mick, right? How'd that go?"

"Great!" Sam replied. "I'm excited about the progress I'm making with the program. I think it's going to be a hit." He paused for a minute as he cleaned up his cutting board.

Realizing he didn't quite answer all of her questions, Virginia asked again, "And lunch with Mick?"

Sam seemed reluctant to answer at first, which piqued her curiosity. "Oh, fine. Yeah. Good. You know Mick. His usual self. What do you want to drink with dinner?" Sam quickly changed the subject.

"Maybe a glass of wine tonight. I'll take the red," she responded, hoping for something to take the edge off and help her relax. She kept watching Sam with increased curiosity as he poured her a glass of Cabernet, wondering why his answer was so vague.

When the meal was finally ready, they sat down at the table to eat. Taking her hand in his, Sam prayed and gave thanks to God for their many blessings. Then, proceeding to coil his spaghetti around his fork, he reluctantly continued, "Mick asked if we would join them for Thanksgiving dinner this year."

Immediately, Virginia understood Sam's reservations in mentioning this earlier. Mick's wife, Leigh, was a contentious woman. She made no apologies for the fact that she disliked Virginia. Family gatherings with her were always filled with angst. So many years had passed since Sam and Virginia's affair and his subsequent divorce. And yet, while they had amicably resolved differences and tried to make amends with those who suffered as a result of their actions, Leigh just could not let it go. Scarlet woman. Jezebel. Hussy. These are just some of the names uttered from Leigh's lips behind Virginia's back and, on occasion, to her face. So, she avoided any such potential conflicts by staying far away from Leigh. Mick, however, was much easier going. "Water under the bridge," he would say. "Pay no mind to her; she'll get over it," he would nonchalantly state. But get over it, she had not. She held it over Virginia's head like a piano being hoisted up the side of a building to a third-floor condo with a fraying rope and pulley—its strands beginning to unravel as an unaware pedestrian walks the sidewalk beneath. That's how Virginia described it, anyhow.

"Ahhh… I see." Virginia calmly replied after taking a few sips of wine. "No wonder you hesitated to tell me about your lunch. How does Leigh feel about this invitation to Thanksgiving? Did

Mick have her blessing to invite us?" Sam was silent. She took his silence as a definitive no.

"Look, Sam. You know I love your cousin. Mick has been nothing short of kind and welcoming to us, especially helping you get settled into your new job. But I'm not going somewhere that I am not welcome. Leigh has made it very clear that she still hates me. I would rather not subject myself to a day of awkwardness and stress during what should be a day of peace and harmony. But if you want to go, I won't stop you. I just can't," her voice trailed off.

"No. Look, it's fine. I'll just tell him we have other plans. Really, Gin, I understand. I hate how she still treats you. She doesn't much care for me either, but tolerates me, I think, because of Mick. No worries. Really, it's cool." Sam reached out his hand to grasp a hold of hers. "She has unresolved issues, and, unfortunately, you get the brunt of it. I'm sorry."

Virginia simply nodded her head. She knew Leigh's backstory. When Leigh was 8 years old, her mother and father got a divorce as the result of her father's torrid affair with a coworker. An ugly custody battle followed, and Leigh, along with her two younger siblings, stayed with their mother, who won sole custody. Her father ended up moving after accepting a new position within his international company's branch office in Spain. The betrayal was hard on Leigh's mother, as she often turned to drinking in excess to ease the hurt. As a result, Leigh and her siblings spent the majority of their time with their grandparents, who practically took on the role of parenting, as Leigh's mother would get sober and then fall off the wagon again. The cycle continued for many years until she was finally open to getting some real help and turning her life around. But by that time, the damage was already done to Leigh's tender soul. So, while it troubled Virginia that Leigh treated her so poorly, she understood. Virginia represented "the other woman" who stole her dad away and caused her life to crumble.

The rest of dinner and evening remained somewhat light in conversation. While Virginia shared the events of her day with Sam, she neglected to share the emotional aspects. The sadness of missing her mom, the flashbacks that paralyzed her in fear amidst the driving rain, and the strange dream that haunted her throughout the day. It was just all weighing on her as she gave Sam a peck on the cheek and retired upstairs for the evening. Crawling into bed and outing the light, Virginia hoped for an uneventful night.

Sam, however, still had some get-up-and-go left in him. He offered to clean up the dishes so Virginia could get an early night. He knew there was something troubling Virginia as she kissed him goodnight. He could see it in her eyes and hear it in her voice. And in the way she pushed the food around on her plate, giving the appearance of eating but clearly not having an appetite. But he had come to know when to press the issue and when to just let

Ginny have some time alone. Tonight, he sensed her need for solitude.

Sam's sensitivity was something that attracted Virginia to him. Not to mention his wit, creativity, and intellect. But there was a gentle way about him that Virginia loved. On the outside looking in, one might say they were the perfect couple. While true that they were a good fit for one another, they certainly weren't perfect. And Sam would be the first to admit that. He was not shy in sharing the gruesome details of his imperfect life when asked. Virginia, on the other hand, preferred to keep those unseemly things under wraps. But Sam was finally at a place in his life where he had made peace with past transgressions and even used his story to help others struggling with similar issues. He knew it would take Virginia more time to face the shadows within, and he was willing to let her contend with spiritual reckoning on her own terms. And in her own time.

CHAPTER 12

All The King's Horses

Sam washed the last pot from dinner and wiped off the stovetop, then decided to catch up on some emails and watch highlights on the national news before calling it a night. As he sat down on the sofa and began to reach for his laptop, he noticed a flower magazine sitting on top of something else on the coffee table. Moving the magazine aside, he saw their wedding album. Sam picked it up and began to leaf through the pages. He began to reminisce about that day. It was a rainy and chilly late October day. And his shoes were too small. *"Man, my feet hurt!"* Sam snickered. But he would have tolerated sore feet time and again to marry Virginia. *"Our anniversary is coming up,"* he thought. *"Eight years already."*

A feeling of warm nostalgia filled Sam's heart as he looked through the pictures, especially upon seeing the photos of Mom and Dad Grey with their arms around both Sam and Ginny. Sam grew very fond of Virginia's parents in the short time they had spent together. He also missed them dearly. Sam turned the page to see his parents proudly standing next to their son. While they did not agree with Sam's divorce and the dishonor of the affair, they let bygones be bygones and agreed to attend the ceremony. Yet another turn of the page made Sam laugh out loud as he saw a candid shot of Willow and Aidan cutting it up on the dance floor.

Turning the pages, one by one, Sam stopped at the picture of Virginia in her off-shoulder wedding gown with delicate beading that shaped her silhouette and laced veil cascading to the floor. She held a bouquet of flowers that she made herself with calla lilies and soft pink roses. *"She's beautiful. I didn't deserve..."* Sam's thoughts were suddenly arrested as he hung on the word "deserve." *"I really don't deserve..."* Once more, the word hit him as if sucker-punched in the gut. Over the years, Sam had dealt with many feelings of inadequacy and worthlessness as he navigated through past childhood wounds and the shame of his former addiction and transgressions. For so long, he hadn't felt worthy or deserving of anything good. Sam began to feel himself spiraling down old, dark tunnels like emotional mineshafts of his soul but shook off the strange sensation as he looked down at the picture of Virginia in her wedding gown once more.

"I've made so many mistakes in my life, but Ginny isn't one of them. She's the best thing that could have happened to me," he

thought as he continued to leaf through the photo album, stopping at another picture of Willow and Aidan, this time with his arms around them as they all posed for the camera. Sam smiled a huge smile of love and pride as his fingers gently traced the outline of the photo. He looked intently at his children's faces, then suddenly became fiercely sober. He began to wrestle with his darker thoughts once more. This time, his thoughts seized the upper hand and subjugated him by force, causing a free-for-all in his mind of negative self-talk and accusations.

"What a joke. I forfeited the best years of my life to an addiction. I can't believe this is my life. What kind of legacy am I leaving for them? I tried so hard to be a good father and still messed up. Why?"

Sam recalled the image of one particular instance. It wasn't long after he and Hannah separated. Sam brought Willow and Aidan back home after taking them out to eat one evening after school. This was part of the agreed-upon arrangement between Sam and Hannah. Upon opening the door, little 9-year-old Willow took off her shoes and tossed them in the corner of the entryway, along with her backpack. Then, bouncing up the staircase to get ready for bed, she stopped at the top step, made an about-face as her long blonde ponytail whirled about her head, and called out below, "Goodbye, Daddy!" And off she went. The image played through Sam's mind as clearly as if it happened just yesterday.

"I became the 'goodbye' dad, not the 'goodnight' dad," Sam self-confessed. "I wasn't there. They deserved so much more. Hannah deserved more. Ginny deserves more!"

Thought after terrible thought, Sam's mind became a warzone of past regrets and remorse. For the last several years, and especially now, since their recent move to Hopeland, Sam tried to remain strong and hold it all together for Virginia's sake. But now, in this unguarded moment, the emotions began to billow from his soul. The inner commotion became unbearable.

"STOP!" he lashed out as he slammed the photo album shut and threw it across the room out of frustration. The album accidentally hit the handmade lighthouse sitting on the coffee table that Daddy Grey made for Virginia, toppling it to the ground. The dread of realizing what he just did mortified Sam. Of all the things he could have broken—it *had* to be Virginia's valued possession of her dad's gifted handiwork.

"No, no, no! NO!" In a panic, Sam rushed over to the floor and began to gather the scattered wooden pieces, then grabbed his head and began weeping the deep tears of lament. Sam wasn't sure how he would explain the broken lighthouse to Virginia, hoping he could fix it by gluing it back together. As he knelt on the floor with pieces in hand, he bitterly recited his modified verse, "All the king's horses and all the king's men couldn't put *my life* back together again…"

Morning light broke through the curtains of the bedroom where Virginia was slowly waking. She was grateful for a solid night's sleep. No weird dreams. No racing thoughts kept her awake at odd hours. Her exhaustion from the previous day's events, along with the glass of wine at dinner, was enough to knock her out for most of the night. She noticed that the sheets on Sam's side of the bed were still fairly neat, so upon making her way downstairs, she discovered Sam sprawled out on the sofa. Virginia knelt next to the sofa, brushed Sam's hair aside, and gently kissed him on the forehead.

"Good morning, sweetie," she whispered in his ear.

Sam grunted slightly, "Already?"

"Yep, already. You never made it up to bed."

"I'm sorry," Sam said as he sat up and rubbed his hand across the back of his neck in an attempt to loosen the kinked muscles that resulted from his emotional night and the hard sofa pillow on which he slept.

"Do you want some coffee?" Virginia offered.

"Yes, please," Sam replied.

Virginia proceeded to the kitchen and began heating some water and grinding up coffee beans for the French Press. Sam shuffled in a couple of minutes later.

"So, what do we do today? Do you have any plans?" Virginia asked.

"No. Not really." His response was short and aloof.

Virginia noticed Sam seemed out of sorts but chalked it up to an uncomfortable night's sleep on the couch. She continued, "Well, it looks like a nice morning if you want to go for a walk. Maybe we can go downtown, and I can show you the building for sale."

Sam shrugged his shoulders and sat down at the kitchen table. "Sure." Again, his reply was blunt.

Virginia brought the French Press and two coffee cups over to the table and sat down. Sam remained quiet. Another minute passed before Virginia spoke out. "Sam, is everything okay? Did I do something to upset you?"

Sam shook his head no but said nothing.

"I don't understand. You seem upset. What is it?" Virginia pressed a bit more assertively. She could see the muscles in Sam's jaw tighten as if he was clenching his teeth. He sighed out loud, then stood up and left the room. "Where are you going?" Virginia called out to him in frustration, not understanding what could have possibly happened between last night and this morning to spark his behavior.

A few minutes passed and Sam still had not returned to the kitchen. Virginia's impatience got the best of her as she got up to find out where Sam went and hopefully find out what was going on with him. She heard a noise in the garage and entered to find Sam opening and slamming cabinet drawers, rifling through their contents.

"Sam, what are you doing? What are you looking for?" Virginia insisted.

"Glue! I'm looking for wood glue. Where is it?"

"I don't know. If it's not in those drawers, maybe it's in one of the toolboxes on the workbench? Why are you looking for glue?" Virginia was very confused at this point, as she watched Sam with concern while his frustration escalated before finally locating the glue in one of the toolboxes.

"Sam, honey, stop!" Virginia's tone caused Sam to look at her, and their eyes met. Virginia could see the look of sadness in his eyes as she drew closer to him. "What's going on?" She asked in a more compassionate voice. Sam's lips began to quiver as he handed her a box containing the lighthouse that he had broken the night before.

"I'm so sorry, Gin. I didn't mean…" Sam broke down.

"Oh no, what happened?" Virginia looked disheartened at the cracked top of the lighthouse and broken pieces of wood that formed the posts and railing surrounding Daddy Grey's nautical creation. Seeing how upset Sam was, Virginia continued, "It's okay, sweetie. Come inside, and we'll talk about it."

Once they settled back at the kitchen table, Virginia poured their coffee as Sam explained how the lighthouse got broken and the emotional and mental triggers that he had experienced the previous night. "It just came out of the blue, Gin. For the most part, I've come to terms with the pain and everything that has happened in my life. But once in a while, I'm just slammed out of nowhere. I know *it is what it is,* and I can't change my past, but when I think about how my choices affected the kids and you... it just overwhelms me. And last night, it felt like all of hell was unleashed against me. I'm so sorry I broke your dad's lighthouse. I'll try to fix it."

"Oh, honey, it's really okay. I know we can fix it, and I'm not worried about that. Sometimes, I get so caught up in my own stuff that I forget you're still healing from everything, too. You're perfectly imperfect, but your kids adore you, Sam. You're a good father and husband." Virginia squeezed Sam's hand. "I love you, always. Look, you had a rough night. Do you just want to stay in today?"

"No. No, I'm okay now," Sam replied. "I want to see the building Maggie showed you. Plus, you're right. It's a nice morning. Let's go for that walk."

"Okay. But first, let's make some pancakes. That always lightens your heart," Virginia grinned. "And I don't know about you, but I could use another cup of coffee."

"Hear-hear!"

CHAPTER 13

Sunday Reflections

*J*t really was a lovely, lazy Sunday morning. Since they were situated in the Bible Belt, most people were still in church services, so the sidewalks were fairly empty. Sam and Virginia took their time and strolled around the park, sitting on the same bench where Virginia met Miss Berti. She then showed him the building for sale in town and explained her vision for the flower shop. Sam was glad to see a spark in Virginia again as she described each and every detail so vividly that he could visualize it all. It had been a long time since he saw her get excited about something. Hopeland was proving to be the right move after all.

Hand-in-hand, they began to make their way back home. "Gin, do you remember how spontaneous we used to be?" Sam asked.

"You mean back when we were youngins," Virginia joked.

"Hey, speak for yourself! I'll be forever young," he poked back.

"Ha!" Virginia laughed. "Well, I remember surprising you when I bought a plane ticket to fly halfway across the country just to see you for one night when you were out of town. I guess that was spontaneous, but I think it was more like stupidity."

"Yeah, you're probably right about that," Sam concurred.

"But then I recall a certain *somebody* who would call me in the middle of the work week and ask if I wanted to go to Philly for dinner. Then you picked me up after work, and we drove two hours to have Pat's cheesesteaks for dinner, walked around the city for a couple of hours, and then drove two hours back home!"

"Wit or wit-out?" Sam mused.

"Definitely wit-out!"

They both laughed as they recalled the tongue-in-cheek way to order a cheesesteak sandwich with or without onions in a Philadelphia accent.

"I can't believe we did that!"

"But it was fun, right? What happened to just picking up and doing something off-the-cuff like that," Sam inquired.

"I guess life got in the way."

"No," said Sam. "I don't think life got in the way. I think we were experiencing life, but then *we* got in the way."

"Hmmm. You're probably right, Sam. Guess we should get out of the way and start living again."

Sam shook his head, "Agreed." Then he raised Virginia's hand to his lips and kissed her as only a gentleman would.

When they got back home, Sam decided to take a quick nap in an attempt to alleviate the grogginess he felt due to his restless night, then do some reading and prepare for the coming week's classes. Virginia took advantage of the down time to act on Miss Berti's suggestion and write down her dream from the previous night. Spending the morning out and about with Sam was a much-needed breath of fresh air. "*It felt good to laugh again,*" she thought as she rummaged through a box in the closet containing some old books and notepads.

Virginia sat down, and, upon opening one of the journals she found in the box, a piece of paper fell to the floor. She picked it up, unfolded it, and began to read. It was Hannah's letter from so many years ago.

"Wow," she said aloud. "I didn't know I kept this." She read it and reread it. The gravity of its message of forgiveness still impacted her heart. She closed her eyes and took a deep breath. "After all these years," she whispered as she refolded the letter and placed it back in the journal.

Virginia began to flip through the pages of her old writings and musings. Some made her smile as she recalled the joy and wonder of her spiritual journey amidst the Heart of the Bride awakening. She read her words of worship penned and titled, "Love's Refrain…"

each element of creation
in passionate congruence
echoes the refrain of my love
across the heavenly expanse...

and joining the Universal Gala
I dance with the sun's rays upon
the glass sea... whose waters
flow to my Beloved's Heart

Tears of remembrance and missing welled up in Virginia's eyes as she read yet another poem, this time written in honor of her parents' relationship in "Legacy of Promise..."

The heart — a resting place for love...
A haven for devotion's poetic declaration
The covenant of two — established in blessing...
Watered with tenderness, yet rooted in strength
Years gone by have seasoned love's utterance...
Years to come will further engrave the legacy of promise.

Others evoked sadness as the words reawakened emotions tied to past hurts. This one, "A Walk in the Rain," reminded her of her recent flashback and getting caught in the rain.

celestial emotion
wells from the gray sky
its steady rain
floods my triune being

droplets of agape
mix with my salty tears
as unabashed they surface
from their reservoir...

to carry the message
of a pained heart

I should fear the dusk
but it comforts me
as gently it wraps me
in its misty blanket

I should look for shelter
but my sanctuary is found here —
within the shower of twilight

And other writings even darker still. She hastily turned to a blank page, then, taking a pen, began writing down her dream.

Virginia finished her journal entry, closed the book, and laid it on her writing desk. Hesitating a moment before walking away, she placed her hand on top of the journal and said a simple prayer. "Abba, I don't know what it means, but if there's something to this crazy dream, I ask you to show me." She then made her way to the kitchen and filled the kettle with water to make a cup of hot tea. Pulling out the basket of assorted teas from the pantry, she rummaged through the boxes to see what might hit the spot. Earl Grey, English Breakfast, Lemon Ginger, Peppermint, Red Rose... "Red Rose it is," she thought. "For you, Mama." With a cup and tea bag in hand, she walked over to the stove to wait for the water to boil. She unwrapped the tea bag from its paper sachet and proceeded to smell the fragrance of its blend of orange pekoe and black tea leaves. Virginia was immediately filled with memories of

Sunday afternoons in Mama Grey's kitchen, sitting around the table in conversation about the weather or what she would be planting in her vegetable garden that year, or sitting outside on her front porch overlooking her prized roses and watching the birds visit the feeder that hung from the eaves. But another memory fought its way to the surface that whisked Virginia away from her present—and took her years into the past to her little Upper West Side apartment.

There was a knock at the door.

"Hi, Mama!" Virginia opened the door to let her mom enter the apartment. Then, giving her a hug, she continued, "Thank you for coming down to help me today. They're gonna knock me out, so I won't be able to drive home."

"Happy to help," Mama Grey replied.

Virginia wasn't looking forward to getting her wisdom teeth extracted, but she was already having some jaw pain. Plus, if it meant not having worse problems later, she'd rather get it taken care of now.

"We have a little bit of time if you want to have a cup of tea before we go," Virginia said as she pulled the chair away from the kitchen table for Mama Grey to have a seat.

"Sounds good, but only if it's *my* tea," she insisted.

"Of course. I always have a stash of Red Rose in my cupboard for you, Mama." Virginia proceeded to get the teacups, sugar container, and milk from the fridge—English style. She was feeling very anxious today, not because of the dental procedure but because she was in over her head with Sam. While she was successful in keeping the affair hidden from those close to her, including her family, she felt like a dam was about to burst inside of her. Secrets were hard for Virginia. Not the kind of secrets where someone is throwing a surprise birthday party, and you have to keep quiet about it, but the kind of secrets that are locked up inside when you've done something wrong or made a grave mistake. The types of things that cause guilt to rise to the surface, like molten lava.

Virginia poured the hot water into the tea cups and sat down with her mom at the small, round glass-top table. Pulling out a small bottle, she explained, "I have to take these pills at least an hour before my appointment, so I don't want to forget. They said it might make me sleepy, so thank you for agreeing to drive." It didn't take long before Virginia felt the effects of the medication. She became very relaxed and very talkative.

Little did Mama Grey know what Virginia was about to divulge. She had no idea what she had walked into that otherwise typical morning. The secret Virginia had been self-containing for months was finally seeping to the surface in an unguarded, sedated moment. Virginia trusted her mom entirely. Though sometimes emotionally reticent and often socially insecure, Mama Grey was the type of person who was consistent, reliable, and protective. She may not have always understood the inner workings of her young, sensitive, and sometimes unconventional daughter, but it was obvious she loved her little girl and was entirely devoted to her family. What Virginia was about to tell her, however, would certainly test that unconditional love.

"Mama, I don't know what to do. I'm in love with a married man." The words spilled out faster than Virginia had time to formulate them. She dared not look up at Mama's face, for surely, she would see disappointment and chagrin.

Up to that point, Virginia lived a careful life, trying to be the perfect girl and live up to expectations—to keep Mama Grey happy and Daddy Grey calm. Virginia's family was more apt to sweep things under the rug than to divulge deep personal feelings about past abuses or youthful indiscretions. But here, in this vulnerable state, she was blurting out her confession—a bomb of astronomical proportions—just minutes before they had to leave for the dental appointment.

Mama Grey maintained composure, took the cup from Virginia's shaking hands, and calmly said, "Ahh, Ginny. Look, we can talk about all that later. Right now, let's get you to your appointment, okay? It'll be alright."

Virginia, feeling quite numb, simply complied and let Mama Grey guide her out of the apartment to the car. They never picked up the conversation again that day, nor did Virginia ask her mom about the impact of her confession—the thoughts and questions racing through Mama's mind as she sat in the waiting room for Virginia to be released. Mama Grey was merely a pillar of strength, going about the task of caring for her daughter and protecting her by holding this newly confessed transgression in confidence until such time as she could pour it out in intercession to God in her prayer closet. That was the measure of a woman that was Mama Grey.

❋ ❋ ❋

"Ginny! Ginny! Hey Gin!!" Sam called out as he rushed into the kitchen and removed the tea kettle from the hot burner as it whistled and billowed steam. "You okay?"

Virginia shook out of her daze. "Oh my gosh, I'm sorry."

"Surely you heard that. It's been going off for about a minute," Sam said as he placed his hand on Virginia's shoulder and got a closer look at her face to assess her condition.

"I'm fine. I'm sorry. I was just deep in thought and... I don't know. I was just somewhere else in my mind."

They sat on the stools at the kitchen island. Sam poured the hot water into Virginia's cup. "Seems like you've been *in your head* a lot these days. Anything you want to talk about?"

"I don't know, Sam. I really don't know what's going on with me lately, but I'm having a lot of recurring memories about my past and about how we got together. I thought all that was behind me when we moved away from New York. One of the reasons I wanted to move here was because there were so many reminders and triggers of things I just wanted to forget about. But it seems to have followed me here."

"Yep. It does that," Sam interjected. "I know that all too well," referring to his recently triggered episode.

"I'm sorry…" she said again, "I don't really want to talk about it now."

"It's okay, Gin. And you don't have to say you're sorry. I'm here if and when you want to talk about it. I just know you've been carrying a lot of weight around on your shoulders for way too many years, and I'm not sure you've really made peace with it all. I'm just worried about you, that's all." Sam left it at that. He could sense Virginia starting to shut down and knew from past experience that he shouldn't press it any further. He kissed her on the cheek and tried to lighten up the mood. "I think I'll make a snack. You want something with your tea?"

"No, thank you. I'll just have the tea." She smiled at Sam with appreciation, removed the teabag steeping in the cup, and held the Red Rose tag between her fingers, fondly recalling the slogan—*A cup'll do you good.* Then, with a sarcastic snicker, she muttered, "I better make it a double!"

CHAPTER 14

Interpretation

The next couple of days presented as calm and uneventful as Virginia finished unpacking the last of the boxes from their move and organized some areas of the house that were in disarray. She certainly loved having everything in its place. It helped her state of mind to have a clutter-free zone at home. As she went about her daily routine, occasionally, she picked up her journal and read over the dream she transcribed— once again praying for some answer or interpretation to it all. Several days had passed since having the dream, and it still lingered with her, nestled in the corners of her mind.

Since Sam was at work and she had the house to herself, she decided to turn on some music and fill the house with singing. She found one of her favorite artists in the stack of CDs she kept. Even though everything was available to stream digitally, she still liked having something tangible to plug in. Turning the volume up a little more than usual, she continued to tidy up the house and hang a few more pictures on the walls, singing and dancing as she worked. All at once, she stopped. And listened. She heard the song a million times before, but this time the lyrics shot out of the speakers and pierced her heart like never before. The words *days of innocence* repeated over and over.

"That's it!" Virginia exclaimed as she fell to her knees. Tears began to flow as the Lord proceeded to reveal the meaning of her dream. It welled up from her spirit like a fountain of healing waters. She rose to her feet and ran to her bedroom, grabbed the journal, and began writing what she perceived to be the interpretation—writing the message in the form of a letter from Abba to Virginia:

My Dearest Virginia,

You feel like your days of innocence were stolen. Before the time you call the Forbidden and which I call your Turning Away, you felt pure and carefree as a child. But then the winds of temptation blew, and, in your weakness, you turned away from Me and leaned into the alluring gale. Yes, you've since returned to Me, and my Mercy is great; my Grace complete. But yet you still carry the shame of your Turning Away as dirty ashes hurled upon the garments of your soul. But I have given you beauty for ashes. You cried out amidst your fall, and I came to your rescue. You are cleansed, my lovely daughter. Through My Sacrificial Lamb, I have restored your innocence and called you by name—Pure. But until you truly embrace this truth, your past transgressions will continue their torment. I desire your freedom and your wholeness. Your past no longer has a hold on you, but you are holding onto it. It may take you some time, but let go of what was, come to Me, and be restored.

I Am… Love, Abba

Virginia laid down her pen and reread what she just penned. Tears once more streamed down her face as she was filled with fresh insight and hope, yet equally shaken by the words. She prayed.

"I don't know how to do this, God. How do I let go of all that happened? It's been so many years since," she paused before calling it the Forbidden and rephrased it, "since my Turning Away. It doesn't seem to bother Sam anymore, and he even helps guys with their issues through what he has been delivered from. But me? I just can't seem to get over it all. You have forgiven me. Hannah has forgiven me, but I… I can't go on like this, Lord. I just can't carry the shame any longer. So, if it means being free once and for all, I'll do it. I'll go wherever you lead and do whatever you ask. But please help me because I'm not as strong as I seem. I'm scared. Thank you, Abba…" Her words trailed off as she sobbed from deep within. As she sat in the stillness for a while longer, she felt an inner peace, giving her strength to face whatever lies ahead.

❊ ❊ ❊

The phone rang. Virginia was composed by this time and answered, "Hello?"

"Ginny? Hi! It's Maggie. Look, sweetie, I have some good news. The sellers are willing to sell at the price we discussed, and they loved hearing about your vision for the place. What do you think? Should we finalize the deal?"

A flurry of excitement filled Virginia as she heard the good news. Could it really be? Her new start? She was silent for a moment as she allowed the possibilities to sink in.

"Ginny? You still there?" asked Maggie.

"Oh, yes. Sorry! I was just taking it all in. That's great news, Maggie. I want to keep things moving, but let me just tell Sam tonight and talk about it. I'll give you a call in the morning. Is that okay?"

"Of course! I'll wait to hear from you then. Have a good night!"

"Thanks, you too!"

Virginia was expecting Sam to be home soon and couldn't wait to share the news. She was filled with hope as she began to think about all the potential and promise the shop held. She threw some soup ingredients in the crockpot and then sat down at the kitchen table with a notebook and pencil and began to jot down ideas and to-do lists. *"There's so much to do!"* she thought as the weight of the decision began to settle. *"No, I'm not going to worry about all that now. One step at a time, Gin,"* she reassured herself as she continued to commit her plans to paper.

Sam showed up about an hour later, and Virginia was still in the kitchen, hashing out all the details for the flower shop. "Gin, hon, I'm home. And we have a visitor."

"In here, Sam," Virginia responded.

Sam entered the kitchen with a teenage boy trailing behind. Virginia guessed his age to be around 16 or 17 but tall for his age. Dark hair, dark eyes, and a mischievous little grin that lit up the room when he entered.

"Ginny, this is Isaac. He's a student from my class, and we're gonna hang out a little tonight if that's okay with you. Isaac has a special part in the musical, so we're going to rehearse a bit."

"Oh, of course. Nice to meet you, Isaac!" Virginia extended her hand towards him.

Still assessing his surroundings and alternating his weight from one foot to the other, Isaac responded in kind and shook Virginia's hand, "Hello, Mrs. Sam."

Virginia laughed. "You're welcome to call me Ginny, but Mrs. Sam will do if you prefer. I have some soup ready if you boys are hungry."

"Sounds great! Then, after we eat, we'll get to work."

During dinner, Virginia told Sam about Maggie's call, and they both agreed to move forward with purchasing the building.

"I'll call Maggie first thing in the morning then," said Virginia.

"Sounds like a plan." Sam paused a minute before continuing, "I know you miss your folks, Gin. And while I know you'd much rather have them here with you now, their inheritance was a beautiful gift to you. You can choose to use it any way you desire. And I think they would be pleased with this choice."

Virginia teared up, "I think you're right, Sam. Thank you." Then, shaking it off, she changed the subject, "Anyone want seconds?"

Virginia cried her share of tears that day and could still feel the rawness of emotions on the brink of overflow, but with their new guest at the table, she purposed to keep it in reserves. She didn't share the interpretation of her dream that she felt came from the Lord earlier that day. She wanted to keep that close and "ponder it in her heart" for a while longer, so she was actually pleased that Isaac was there as a distraction.

After dinner, Sam and Isaac went into the living room as Virginia cleaned up the dishes. She was amused to hear them rehearsing Isaac's special part for the outreach program, as Sam would sing a line of the chorus and Isaac would echo, "We are the reason…" Then they would break out in belly laughs as one or the other messed up or made a joke. Virginia loved the sound of laughter filling the home. Something seemed familiar about Isaac's name, so she grabbed her Dictionary of Bible Names from the bookshelf and looked up Isaac—"*He will laugh. How fitting,*" she thought as she watched them interact with one another in the adjacent room. Isaac's laughter brought joy to Virginia's otherwise heavy heart. And so, she joined them... and sang along... and laughed.

Mother of Many

Friday morning came and Virginia was getting ready to meet Maggie to go over last minute details for closing on the property. Then, she was off to see Berti again at the Cinnamon Shack for their weekly tea date. She was looking forward to sharing the dream interpretation she received and was thankful there was no rain in the forecast.

Maggie was her usual bubbly self.

"Maggie, I think you are more excited about this transaction than I am," Virginia joked.

"You know it!" Maggie exclaimed. "There are some sales that just feel right, and Ginny, dear, this feels so right! The moment you shared your vision with me, I could see its fulfillment right here at the corner of Hopeland. And I am going to be one of your first customers. You can count on that!"

"Thank you, Maggie. You've been so great through all of this. I'd love to keep in touch. Maybe after things settle down a bit, you can come over for dinner sometime? Actually, if you're not busy around the holidays, I'd love to have you over then."

"That would be perfect, Ginny! You just let me know when, and I'll be there."

"Great. I will be in touch then. And, Maggie, truly, I am so grateful for your help. You're a gem!"

"Awww… it's been a pleasure. Now, I'll give you a call when the papers are all ready to sign and we'll seal this deal," Maggie said as she gave Virginia a big hug.

This is really happening. Virginia was so excited to get started on fixing up the place and making it her own. But she was equally nervous about embarking on this new adventure. So much was happening and so quickly. Virginia's mind was still spinning with ideas as she opened the door of the Cinnamon Shack. Sure enough, there was Miss Berti sitting at the same table with a fresh pot of hot water and two cups in place just waiting. She waved at Lois before making her way over to the table.

"Ginny! Oh, it's so good to see you again," Berti sang out.

"Likewise, Miss Berti. Have you been waiting long?"

"Oh, no. You're right on time. I was just here early. Brought a book along to read."

"Did you finish that one you had in the park when we first met? The Beverly Lewis book?"

"Oh yes. Just finished it the other day. Such a good story. Do you like her books?"

"I honestly haven't had a chance to read many of them, but my mom loved them. That's how I knew about the author."

Virginia poured herself a cup of tea, and the two chatted about random topics before Virginia told her the good news about buying the building for her flower shop. She told her all about her plans to fix it up, the design ideas she had in mind, and the flowers she wanted to start bringing in from growers. Eventually, she hoped to work with some flower markets in the area and even start growing her own in the spring.

"Oh, Ginny, that's such wonderful news. I'm so very happy for you." Berti was genuinely interested. "You seem in better spirits today, yes?"

Virginia smiled, "Yes. It's been quite a week, though. Remember that dream I had? And what you encouraged me to do last time we met?"

Berti grinned from ear to ear. "I do. And did you ask Abba?"

"I did, Miss Berti. I wrote it down in my journal and prayed about it."

"And did He answer?" Berti inquired.

"He did. You know how sometimes you don't get answers to things you pray about for a long time? Well, within a few days He revealed to me what I believe to be the interpretation."

"Do you wish to share it with me? There is no need to if it's something between you and Abba. But it's up to you." Berti was the gentlest soul Virginia had ever met. She was so comfortable and easy to talk to.

"It's a bit of a long story, Miss Berti. Maybe I'll fill you in on the backstory another time, but I'd love to share what Abba gave me."

Virginia proceeded to share the interpretation but left out the full explanation and details of the Forbidden, the Turning Away. She simplified it by stating that she had gone through an ordeal that was difficult and inappropriate and turned away from God during that time. But Berti could fill in the blanks and wasn't naïve. She knew exactly what Virginia was referring to but didn't pry or let on. She simply listened intently.

When Virginia concluded, Berti took her hands, held them, and began praying, "Oh, Abba, how beautiful. Thank you for revealing the secrets of the heart in such a glorious way to your daughter, Ginny. You are good."

"You are truly a remarkable woman, Miss Berti. I'm glad I shared a bench with you that day."

"Me too, dear. Me too!" Berti responded.

Just then, the door to the café opened and in poured a mom and her two little toddlers—one dressed in pink and the other in blue.

"Oh, my word," Berti remarked. "She has her hands full with those two little ones. And twins, I believe!"

"They're adorable," said Virginia as she watched the two little bundles of energy climb under and over chairs and make figure eights in and around mom's legs. She sighed deeply as she watched the children… smiling, yet a sad longing filled her eyes.

Berti noticed and delicately advanced. "I think you mentioned that you had no children. Is that right?"

"That's right, Miss Berti. None of my own. I have two stepchildren, though—Willow and Aidan. They're awesome kids. Here, I have pictures of them on my phone."

"Oh, they're simply gorgeous. Almost all grown up now, I see."

"Yes. I sometimes wonder where the time has gone."

"Tell me about it," Berti kidded.

After a good laugh, Virginia got serious again. "I've never been able to conceive. We tried for many years, but the doctor said the test results confirmed my barrenness."

"That must have been so difficult for you, Ginny. I, too, was not able to have children. It's a profound heaviness to carry in your heart as a woman, I know."

The two sat in silent understanding for a few minutes, sipping their tea and watching as the mom corralled her little ones and settled them down at the corner table to drink their glasses of milk while she enjoyed a cup of coffee.

Virginia looked at her watch. "Same time, same place next week, Miss Berti?"

"Quite right. It will be the highlight of my week." Berti rose from her chair to give Virginia a hug.

"Same here," Virginia replied. "And today is on me. I'll settle up with Lois on my way out."

With a lightened heart, Virginia paid the tab and waved goodbye as she declared, "See you next week!"

The following days were filled with Internet research and fact-finding for Virginia as she tried to find resources, make connections with local growers, and develop a network of wholesalers for her products. Both Virginia and Sam had a lot to accomplish in the coming weeks. And soon, the holidays would be upon them. As Virginia returned from running errands one afternoon, she opened the door to find an envelope on the floor that apparently someone slipped through the mail slot. On the front was her handwritten name. Filled with curiosity, Virginia placed her bags on the kitchen counter, opened the envelope, and read from the card inside.

Dearest Ginny,

You may not have borne your own children in the natural, but you will in the spiritual. A verse that has blessed me over the years.

Rejoice, childless woman, who does not give birth. Burst into song and shout, you who are not in labor, for many are the children of the desolate... (Isaiah 54:1)

May it encourage you as well. Love, Berti!

Virginia clasped the card to her chest and stood for a few minutes, allowing the message to sink in. She had never thought about that before—spiritual children? She always thought her infertility was a curse, but could it have been a blessing in disguise? She recalled various relationships in her life where she was a mother figure of sorts to younger women who were going through difficult times. She never saw herself as a "mother" in a spiritual context, but in hindsight, she had to agree with the premise.

"Wow," Virginia breathed deeply. "Thank you, Miss Berti. You always know just what to say."

Just then, Sam entered the room. Virginia wasn't trying to hide the note, but she instinctively slid the card under a stack of papers. Perhaps she just wasn't ready to share it with anyone yet. She needed more time to ponder its meaning.

"Hey, hon! You're back. I wanted to ask if you would mind having Isaac over again this week. It's actually a sad story. I knew his family life was less than stellar, but this new development shines light on a lot of things. His father just got picked up for possession of child pornography."

"Oh, no, Sam!"

"Yeah, it's not good. I don't think Isaac knows any details about it, but even so, things are going to be stressful at home, and I just really want to be a safe place for him right now. Is that okay with you?"

Virginia's mind immediately went to the note. *Many are the children of the desolate...* "Of course," she affirmed. "He is welcome here any time. I really like Isaac. His laugh is contagious. Sam, I don't recall if you told me what Isaac's disability is. Is he a high-functioning autistic?"

"Actually, there was a childhood accident that resulted in a traumatic brain injury. And you're right, he has a great laugh!"

"Our home is his home as long as he needs. He's lucky to have you in his life," Virginia hugged Sam.

"Well, I don't know about that," Sam teased, "but my heart really goes out to his dad, too. If he gets any jail time, I might try to arrange a visit with him. While my addiction may not have escalated to the point of viewing child pornography, I still understand the underlying struggle. He needs some serious counseling. I don't know how they are going to handle his situation legally, but it's going to be a difficult road no matter what."

"Yes, it will. You're a good man, Sam Novak. Helping to comfort those with the comfort you have received. I'm proud of you."

Sam simply grinned before changing the subject. "On another very important note, Mrs. Novak, there's a very special day coming up."

"Oh?" Ginny teased, knowing full well what he was talking about. "And what would that be, Mr. Novak?"

"Well, I know things have been a bit hectic since we moved here, but what do you say to dinner and a movie this weekend to celebrate our anniversary? Mick told me of a couple of really nice restaurants in the area."

"What, no four-hour round trip spontaneous excursion to grab a Philly cheesesteak?" Virginia joked.

At that, Sam heartily laughed. "Hmmm… maybe another time. How about we settle for a twenty-minute drive for Italian?"

"È Perfetto!"

CHAPTER 16

Thankful Heart

The weeks flew by with a flurry of activity. Settlement occurred on the shop and was officially in Virginia's ownership. Paint supplies and curtains were already purchased, and Virginia had already spent a few days cleaning the shop and preparing it for a face lift. Sam continued his rehearsals with the students for their annual outreach program, as costumes and sets were being amassed in their living room. Isaac was a regular in the Novak home. Virginia continued to meet Berti every Friday afternoon without fail—the highlight of her week. And Thanksgiving was quickly approaching.

"So, Mick called me again," Sam carefully navigated the topic while making breakfast. "He was wondering if we've made plans for Thanksgiving yet?"

"I see. Look, Sam, I've been thinking about that recently. Even though it might be awkward with Leigh, I know it's important to be with family at Thanksgiving. And since we can't travel up north to be with the kids and to see my side of the family, Mick is the closest family we have. I can handle Leigh's attitude and snide remarks for one day. Go ahead and accept his invitation. And when you talk to him, ask what we can bring, okay?"

"Are you sure, Gin? We can leave early if it gets too crazy. But I think it would mean a lot to Mick if we were there."

"It's fine. I'm sure." Virginia tried to sound cheerful, but she was still uncomfortable with the idea. Yet this was another one of those areas in which she wanted to embrace the truth Abba spoke to her and let go of the stigma of her past. She knew the Lord would give her strength to get through Thanksgiving and had come to realize that whatever issues Leigh had with her were just that—Leigh's issues, not hers.

With broccoli casserole and apple crumble in hand, Sam and Virginia knocked on Mick and Leigh's door adorned with a cornucopia wreath and welcome sign.

"We'll see how welcome we are," Virginia said under her breath to Sam. He just shot her a sarcastic look.

"Sam! Ginny! Happy Thanksgiving! Come on in," Mick answered the door in full-blown festive attire—burnt orange and yellow sweater with fall leaves and pumpkins and what appeared to be a dancing turkey—and demeanor to match, followed by a huge bear hug.

"Good morrow, Sir Michael. How fare thee?" Virginia bantered.

"Well met, my lady. Pray, enter," Mick jumped right into character.

"Oh, brother," Sam sighed and rolled his eyes. They all burst into laughter.

"Thanks for inviting us, Mick. Where would you like me to put these?" Virginia asked as she extended her hands, holding a dish.

"Here, give it to me, and I'll take it to the kitchen. Dinner won't be long, so make yourself comfy. There are some drinks on the table over there, and the kids are watching the National Dog Show on TV, I think." Mick always made people feel at ease, and Virginia was grateful for that.

Mick's teenage girls were stretched out on the sofa and waved hello as Sam and Virginia entered the room. The house smelled and looked like Thanksgiving, for sure. The family room was decorated with strings of fall leaves, pilgrim figurines, and pictures with thanksgiving-inspired words such as "Give Thanks," "Be Grateful," and "Gather Together." Virginia glanced into the dining room and saw the table all decked out with the best linens and table settings. Leigh always had to put on her very best.

"Can I help with anything?" Virginia called out to the kitchen.

Leigh's voice rang out immediately, "No. I've got it all under control." Virginia understood immediately.

The next couple of hours were pleasant enough. Leigh's side of the family showed up, including her younger brother and his two little boys, and the volume immediately turned up to eleven. Virginia enjoyed bantering with Mick; hearing the girls chatter about school, friends, and, of course, boys; and watching the young lads across the table as they plotted their after-dinner mischief. Leigh joined in the conversation but rarely looked in Virginia's direction. Virginia wasn't put off, as she didn't expect the welcome mat from Leigh to begin with. But all in all, dinner was delicious, and her apple crumble was a hit.

People began to withdraw from the dining room table and head to the family room to either watch football or take a nap, and Virginia decided to help clean up some dishes from the table. Gathering a couple of plates and silverware, she started to walk towards the kitchen but stopped at the doorway as she overheard Leigh's conversation with Mick.

"Look, I'm still not okay with what they did and they just act like nothing ever happened. She's a home-wrecker, Mick. You know full well that I didn't want to invite them, and yet you still asked them. Are you even sure she's a good influence around the kids? I mean, wasn't she admitted to the psych ward at one point?" Leigh's words were sharp and cutting.

Mick, clearly perturbed at what his wife just said, spoke up in defense. "Come on, Leigh! How can you even say that? What she went through during that time was her own business. Sam and

Ginny are good people. Sure, they messed up, but they've all made peace with it and have moved on. You need to get over it, Leigh! Your hostility towards Ginny is misdirected, and you know it!"

The sound of a spoon falling from Virginia's grip to the floor disrupted their kitchen quarrel. She quickly picked it up and, pretending that she wasn't privy to their conversation, entered the kitchen and chose to heap coals of fire as kindness upon the situation. "Dinner was fantastic, Leigh. I couldn't eat another bite! Thank you so much for having us over. Let me wash up the dishes for you so you can go put your feet up and enjoy your family. I insist."

Leigh's face turned flush with embarrassment. She humbly accepted the offer and went into the family room. Mick, sighing loud enough for Virginia to hear, quietly apologized, "I'm sorry, Ginny. Thank you."

"No problem. Oh, Mick, can you ask Sam to come in with me, please?"

Virginia's hands were trembling as the harshness of Leigh's words began to plunge a little deeper into her heart. Sam entered the kitchen, noticed her distress, and hugged her as she stood at the sink. "You wanna talk about it?"

She wiped a single tear from her cheek, "No. Not right now. But can we get out of here?"

"Of course," Sam reassured her.

Loading the last dish into the dishwasher, Sam and Virginia gathered their stuff, thanked their hosts for a lovely meal, and gracefully bailed out of the remainder of the celebrations.

The car ride home was quiet as Sam and Virginia simply held hands and listened to soft music in the background. Virginia tried to redirect her wandering thoughts, but it was a battle the entire car ride. Closing her eyes she offered a quiet prayer, *"Abba, help me to have a thankful heart. Thankful for what you've brought us through and for what is yet to come."*

Upon arriving back home, Virginia asked Sam if they could just talk later about everything, as she just wanted to take something for her pounding headache, lie down, and hopefully get some rest. Sam, of course, understood and gave her the space she needed. He decided to watch an old movie and veg out for a few hours anyhow, but, in all reality, he'd probably fall asleep after eating so much at Thanksgiving dinner.

Virginia took something to help ease her headache, closed the shades to the bedroom, and reclined in bed. She tried to continue to push the negative thoughts away, but Leigh's words cut deep. The phrase, *"Wasn't she admitted to the psych ward..."* continued to play like a broken record in her mind. That wasn't normally something she talked about, and for the longest time, she was ashamed of the whole ordeal. She actually didn't realize that news of her involuntary commitment to the psychiatric unit of the hospital (or a "302" as it is known in the medical industry) reached

Mick and Leigh. She was hoping it remained in the confines of immediate family and some close friends. So, hearing Leigh mention it with such disdain struck a nerve in Virginia. Not able to rest, she went over to the desk, picked up her journal, sat down by the window, and began to read.

CHAPTER 17

Rest In Peace

*J*ournal entry, March 2002, entitled R.I.P.

the silence is harrowing here...
and it is cold, very cold
the final heap of soil has been hurled
upon my corpse
the last pat of the death spade
seals my sentence from above
this is my verdict...
this is my fate...
buried alive
left only with the memories
that torment for eternity
memories...
whose anguish will be the means
of my suffocation... not the impacting earth
that crushes my lungs, stealing my breath
but the memories
of lost love...
of broken dreams...
of the forbidden

grave-keepers plant flowers
to adorn the crypt of my remains
yet the petals fall, and the greens wither...
only the thorns survive, absorbing the bitter potion
that seeps from my decaying carcass
and the passersby shiver
as they near my memorial...
seized by the vexed soul
that "rests in peace" below

Virginia recalled the void of the dark season that led up to the writing of this particular journal entry. Once again, she found herself swallowed up in a series of flashbacks—the flood of memories playing before her as scenes in a movie.

❀ ❀ ❀

9/11. The day the earth stood still... and Virginia's personal world fell apart. It was in the thick of the Forbidden... the Turning Away. She had a hair appointment that day, and Sam was waiting for her back at the apartment where they were going to spend the day together. While at her hair appointment, the news of the terrorist attack at the World Trade Center's twin towers was erupting. Such a horrendous scene! Everyone in the salon was terrified, calling loved ones to make sure they were safe. Reports of crashing planes and falling buildings shot fear into the hearts of all.

But for Sam, the events unfolding before him struck a particularly alarming chord. He was convinced that it was the end of the world and that judgment was coming upon mankind. An overreaction? Perhaps. But he was living in such fear of God because of his sinful lifestyle—the affair and his pornography addiction—that rational thinking was not the prevailing norm. So, in a state of panic, Sam left Virginia's apartment and went back *home* to Hannah and the children in repentance—to make things right in the eyes of God. Virginia returned to the apartment to find a note hastily written on the coffee table:

Ginny,

God's judgment has come. I have to go back to make things right. I'm sorry for all the pain I have caused you.

Sam

Anguish engulfed Virginia in an instant. Her already fragile world turned upside down. Even though she knew the horrific events unfolding in the news were incomparably worse than what was happening to her, she felt in that moment that she, too, crumbled as the Twin Towers that day. She was devastated, hysterical, and strangely felt like *she* was now the one betrayed.

Virginia didn't know what to do or where to turn. She isolated herself so much during the affair that she felt she had no one to run to. Certainly not God! And if not God, then who? Virginia called Sam's cell phone a hundred times, and with every unanswered call, she felt even more adrift.

The days that followed were spent trying to make sense of all that just happened. How could she return to a life of "normalcy" after all that had transpired? Virginia was not the same person she once was. And she didn't know who she had become.

The magnetism between Sam and Virginia was too strong to break. With each passing day that they were apart, the door they attempted to weld shut began to crack open again. And before long, Sam broke the silence with another phone call.

"Hi."

"Hi."

There it was again—that one-syllable, two-letter word that brought with it the monumental force of burning emotion. And even though Sam still resided with Hannah in an attempt to reconcile, his connection resumed with Virginia.

And then the holidays arrived.

Christmastime. A season Virginia loved more than any other— a time of great memory, wonder, and tradition in the Grey family came and went with barely a recollection for Virginia. She was not whole. She was splintered. And numb. Her mind and heart were elsewhere, yet her body was going through the expected routine of holiday traditions.

The Grey family went all out at Christmas. The jolly celebrations began early on Christmas Eve day as the kitchen was bustling with cooking and baking while Christmas music blared in the background. Last-minute Christmas present wrapping would take place upstairs behind closed doors, away from prying eyes. Meanwhile, children played with the train set around the

Christmas tree and snuck cookies from the baking trays fresh out of the oven when no one was watching. After Christmas dinner, the Grey clan donned their best Christmas attire for church candlelight service, followed by music and caroling, and then the real fun began. As the hour neared midnight, Daddy Grey would pile all the kids in the car and go on a search for Rudolph's shining red nose in the sky. Excited children bounced back and forth in their seats, peering out the windows to point out every blinking red light they could see. Then, upon arriving home, sure enough, Saint Nick had arrived, as was evident by the presents adorned under the tree. This tradition was observed for generations in the Grey family and was always a joyous time for all—children and adults alike. However, for Virginia this year, the usual Yuletide festivities lost their luster as she went through the motions, feeling empty and detached. Yet no one noticed.

New Year's Eve. Virginia reservedly accepted an invitation to a co-worker's house to bring in the New Year. She and Sam were still communicating, and she told him where she would be that evening. She thought for certain he would call her or surprise her by showing up at the party where she was "celebrating" (rather, "commiserating"). But with every minute that passed, as the midnight hour drew nigh, Virginia was excruciatingly disappointed as she realized Sam was not going to show up. Once more, her heart was sickened by disappointment, and the raw ache of loneliness accompanied her as she drove home—car lights passing by, but she was barely aware of them as she stared blankly at the road ahead.

Virginia didn't sleep much that night… lying on her bed in the darkness, haunted by the critter that she assumed was a mouse scratching in the insulation of her bedroom ceiling, trying to escape the cold winter night. Between sobs, she cursed and hurled every obscenity she knew at the little varmint—just wishing it would die! Yet the sound of every scratch from its sharp claws grew louder and louder. It was in the early hours of that melancholy night that Virginia sat at her computer with a bottle of Jack Daniels in hand and began to type her first suicide note.

> *If I can't be with the man I love, what's the use? How do I live without him? I've given him everything… all of myself… and now, I have nothing left. I have nowhere to turn. I can't live with the mess I've made. This pain is too much. I'm so, so sorry…*

Irrational compositions of words and phrases gushing from a wounded and confused heart. It was this heart that foolishly bought into the perverted narrative spun by romantic happily-ever-after movies and twisted Romeo & Juliet "I'd rather be with you in death than go on living without you" plots.

The self-inflicting weapon of choice to end her despair was the set of knives in her kitchen. Virginia had a very weak stomach when it came to all things medical. Her high empathic gift made it difficult for her to even hear stories of accidents or details of surgery. If a person described an injury or medical procedure to her, she instantly felt the pain in her body and became flush with a wave of heat to the point of passing out if she didn't quickly remove herself from the earshot of the storyteller. So, the very thought of cutting herself terrified her. But she didn't know how else to "get the deed done." Frantically, she drank more liquid courage to overcome the fear.

Virginia never did muster up the "courage" to cut herself. She passed out on the kitchen floor with the knife lying on the ground next to her. God stayed her hand and saved her life that day. But this, unfortunately, was not the last of her suicide attempts.

Virginia and Sam resumed an "off and on again" relationship once more, even after he tried to go back and make his marriage with Hannah work. The constant push-and-pull started to become too much to bear, as Virginia was being crushed under the weight of it all. She just wanted closure—for Sam to make a choice, so she would no longer be in the place of constant relational limbo.

In the wee hours of a cold March night, Virginia was overtaken by an irrational impulse. In order to force herself to follow through with this crazy plan, she called for a taxi to take her to Sam's house. If she had driven her own car, she may have gotten there, chickened out, and driven back home. The taxi driver dropped Virginia off at Sam's residence, and knowing that he parked his vehicle along the street, she decided to sleep in Sam's car until he came out in the morning in order to confront him—to give him an ultimatum. Her plan, however, was not carefully planned out. Otherwise, she would have taken a warm blanket or pillow along to make her camping out in the cold vehicle more tolerable. She may have dozed off a few minutes here and there, but for the most part, Virginia sat staring into the night sky, running through various scenarios of how it would all play out in a few hours. What would she say to him? How would he react? A predictable outcome was inconclusive. She would have to wait and see. And wait, she did.

To say that Sam was surprised to see Virginia curled up in the front seat as he opened the door to his car to climb in would be an understatement. Sam did not greet her with excitement but rather with confusion and frustration.

"What the—!!" Sam yelped. "Ginny, what the heck are you doing here?"

"Honestly, I don't know. I've been here all night trying to figure out what I was going to say to you," Virginia replied.

"Look," Sam said, in a matter-of-fact voice, "I'm late for work. I have to go."

"Well, then, let's go because I'm not getting out until you hear what I have to say," Virginia insisted.

"Fine." Sam was curt. It was obvious that he didn't like being caught off balance like this. And how could Virginia really blame him? He was, after all, gasping for his next breath in the midst of his own hellish flood while Virginia's surprise confrontation plunged his head further under the torrent.

As Sam started to drive, Virginia began her ultimatum. "Sam, I don't think you understand what this is doing to me. I'm being torn in two. One minute, we're together, and the next, we're not. I just can't live like this anymore. So, you need to choose. Are you going to leave and be with me? Or are you going to stay and be with her? Because you can't have both!"

Her demands might as well have fallen on deaf ears. Sam was in no frame of mind to discuss the matter, nor was he capable of making such an impossible choice. The *right choice*, according to what he knew in scripture, would be to stay with Hannah and continue to *try* to make it work for the sake of the kids. But that would mean rejecting Virginia, who truly felt like his home, his true north. He couldn't bear the thought of losing what he found in Virginia. But, likewise, he couldn't bear the thought of abandoning his children. The demand for a decision was impossible to meet.

Sam sat dumbfounded, unable to speak, which made Virginia furious. "So, that's it. Nothing. You have nothing to say!"

"What do you expect me to say, Ginny? I'm just trying to survive here! I can't do this right now!"

"Whatever. Stop the car! Stop the car and let me out!" Virginia cried.

Sam stopped at the next traffic light, and without thought or warning, Virginia jumped out of the car and slammed the door behind her. This particular outcome was not one she had considered. She ran as fast as she could, sobbing uncontrollably, and didn't turn back to see whether or not Sam followed her or drove away. When she stopped running, Virginia found herself in the midst of a cemetery. She practically fainted from the emotional and physical exhaustion, and the reality of the thirty-degree winter air now set in as Virginia began to shiver from the cold. While feeling completely dispirited and empty, she felt a strange belonging as she crumpled to the ground and leaned against the nearest tombstone, trying to disappear. The dropping of her tears became a steady dirge of grief to the graves beneath. Virginia couldn't recall how she got home that day, only that she felt a part of her remained buried in that cemetery—R.I.P.

Suicidal ideation was pervasive during this dark time, as Virginia tried to think of ways she could end the pain. But with each passing day, she would try to convince herself to make it through one more day. And so, one more day came and went... ever slowly creeping along... one by one. Each day was muddled with hours and hours of unending malaise. Her suicide attempts were not temper tantrums because she couldn't have what she wanted, but an act of despising herself for wanting what she shouldn't have. She felt dirty, unworthy, unwanted, lost... and felt so much pain that she just wanted it all to end. So, after almost a year of personal chaos, she finally decided to take more serious measures. Enough was enough. She was really going to end things this time.

It was late one winter night when, with a Xanax pill bottle in hand, Virginia decided on suicide by overdose. She methodically counted out the pills to make sure she had enough to do the trick.

"1, 2, 3, 4… 10, 11, 12… 23, 24… 28. Surely that will do it. Now, what to down them with?" The only alcohol she could find in the apartment was a bottle of champagne. Champagne—the celebratory beverage of choice for most was now to be her farewell potion. Once she gathered her lethal concoction, she quickly downed them before she could talk herself out of it. The dosage, however, was not fatal. Instead, the Xanax/champagne cocktail resulted in extreme sedation that impaired her cognition and caused her to behave like the walking dead.

It wasn't long before the mixture took effect, and soon Virginia was unaware of even her own actions. She fumbled around her desk and found a pad of sticky notes, then began to scribble messages to family members and friends, and even to God, apologizing to them for her actions and for all the hurt and disappointment she may have caused them. She left these sticky notes along her path like breadcrumbs as she proceeded to stumble down the staircase to locate her keys. As she was leaving the apartment, she grabbed a few items of significance before staggering out the door—a CD and a mini book.

The CD was a worship album that was *so* instrumental (no pun intended) during her Father's Heart experience at her home church years ago. She must have played it a thousand times in worship as she sought the Father's heart in days gone by.

The second item was a tiny book of old gospel hymns that belonged to Sam but that she confiscated as her own because she loved it so much. The book, with its beautifully worn and aged cover and pages, was over 100 years old and contained only the words of 233 new sacred songs and standard gospel hymns, yet small enough to fit into your pocket. Even in her present state of mind, Virginia's spirit was still reaching out to heaven in hopes that God would have mercy on her. Subconsciously, she knew God was the answer, but she couldn't find her way out of the hellish pit she fell into. How telling were those objects that she wanted near her at the "end."

Virginia climbed into her car and drove aimlessly down the road barely at turtle speed and bouncing off guardrails along the way. It's a miracle that she wasn't involved in a serious accident where someone could have been hurt or even killed. She must have driven at least ten miles before a driver who witnessed her erratic driving called the authorities. A state police officer was soon on the scene and brought her car to a halt. It wasn't long before he realized Virginia was not in her right mind and was obviously under the influence of something. What, though, he didn't know. Between sobs and upchucks and with slurred speech, Virginia poured out her lament to the officer about how she made terrible mistakes, that she hated the person she had become, and how so very sorry she was for everything. Once the ambulance arrived on the scene, she was rushed to the Emergency Department. At the hospital, she was treated for an overdose and admitted for clinical depression.

Virginia's hospital experience was quite an interesting ordeal. It was another world altogether! Initially, she didn't have much recollection, as the mixture she ingested a few hours earlier was still yielding its effects. Yet in a hazy memory, she remembered lying on a table as the Emergency Room doctor was examining her, looking up at the doctor and stating, "Has anyone ever told you that you look like Keanu Reeves?" Apart from having dark brown hair and eyes that matched its hue, Virginia wasn't sure he looked anything like the famous actor. But the moment of levity was welcomed nonetheless.

As a result of her suicide attempt, Virginia was involuntarily admitted as a "302" to the inpatient psychiatric ward of the hospital for five days. Once the effects of the sedation wore off, she was in complete shock at her present circumstance. *"How did I get here!? I don't belong in this place. These people are seriously ill, and yet, I am one of them... treated like a nutcase."* It was a pill harder to swallow than the 28 pills she took to get there.

The worst part was the nights. Sleeping was almost impossible. The first night, Virginia was in a room by herself and had some privacy as the influence of the overdose cleared her system. But then she was moved in with a roommate. A very odd and troubled soul was she. Virginia remembered thinking that this roommate had some very evil demons tormenting her, for the atmosphere surrounding her was dark and wicked. She would blurt out random cuss words into the air as if directed toward someone... or something. In an attempt to escape her torment, Virginia found the woman crushing her evening dosage of medication and snorting it, thinking no one was around to witness her actions. If it wasn't the flailing and mumbling sounds coming from her roommate at night, it was the periodic room checks by staff who shined their flashlights in her face to make sure she was still there and okay. Well, Virginia was there. But she certainly was *not* okay.

Group sessions were always something to look forward to. There were special activities, discussions on health and nutrition, or relaxation and meditation sessions.

Close your eyes... envision a place that makes you feel...

safe... and happy... Feel your body relax...

your head, face, neck, shoulders...

moving down your arms...

And the exercise continued for the next thirty minutes. Virginia embraced those moments because it was one of the rare times in her confinement that it was quiet. No buzzing noises or alarms, no emotional outbursts from patients, no nurses raising their voices to get someone's attention, no one pacing back and forth talking to themselves. Here, during the meditation session, perhaps the occasional cough or creak from a chair. But otherwise, quiet. She relished those moments.

The days progressed at an excruciatingly slow pace. However, after a couple of days, a sense of comradery began to develop with some of the other patients as they shared their individual stories. Virginia started to come out of herself and began to feel compassion for others and their struggles.

Among the nursing staff on the ward, Virginia became known as the Champagne and Xanax girl, as if that were the classiest attempt at suicide they had ever heard. While, in retrospect, Virginia understood their tongue-in-cheek remarks, she was not laughing at the time, nor did she intend her suicide attempt to be elegant in any manner.

It's been said that suicide is a selfish act. And generally speaking, Virginia supposed that was true. But when she was contemplating suicide, she was not taking anything else into consideration other than the chaos inside. In order for the pain to stop, she saw no other solution. She was blinded to any other alternative. She shamed her God! She was a failure. Surely, even He wouldn't rescue her from her own destruction. She wanted the tormenting thoughts to cease. She wanted the gut-wrenching pain that took her breath away to stop. She just wanted to Rest In Peace.

CHAPTER 18

Skandalon

By the time Virginia snapped out of her flashback of deep and dark recovered memories, Sam was entering the bedroom. Virginia was curled up in a ball on the chair, holding her face in her hands. Sam came to her side and gently touched her shoulder. Her face turned upwards as she looked at him, and the surge of tears burst forth. Sam knelt next to her and held her as the cleansing wave of emotion flowed; then, when it subsided, he gently inquired.

"Ginny, honey, what's going on? Please talk to me."

"I don't know how to put it all in words. It's so much, Sam."

"Just try," he encouraged.

"I've been carrying so much unresolved crap around from my past for years and years. Mostly from when, rather *how*, we got together. The affair and its consequences. My suicide attempts in the midst of that horrible time. Then my inability to have children and trying to figure out how to be a good stepmom to Willow and Aidan. Dealing with how your addiction impacted me, even though I was clueless at the time. And losing my parents." Her voice shook as she took a minute to speak again. "I thought moving away from New York would make it easier, but it followed me here, Sam. I keep having flashbacks and memories of it all. Then today Leigh…"

"I knew it. What did she say, Gin?" Sam got protective.

"I just overheard her talking to Mick in the kitchen. She called me a home-wrecker and was worried how I would negatively influence her kids, bringing up the fact that I was, in her words, in the psych ward. How did she find out anyhow? That's a really sensitive subject for me, Sam. You know that. It still all just hurts so much."

"Oh, Ginny. I'm so sorry. Look, I'll talk to Mick. We're not going over there again," Sam said sternly.

"No, no. Don't say anything right now. It's just that, along with everything else I've been feeling lately, it cut pretty deep today. Sam, how do you do it? All the things you've gone through. You went to hell and back, and yet you are able to talk about your past with ease, it seems. I know you still have times when you're triggered, but it seems like it doesn't bother you in the same way. Why can't I get over it, Sam? The Lord has been dealing with me lately to let things go. I'm trying, but why is it so hard?"

Virginia continued to share with Sam the dream she had several weeks ago and the interpretation the Lord gave her. She also shared the flashbacks she'd been having, the conversations with Miss Berti, and the encouraging card she sent with the scripture. She shared it all.

"Look, Gin, all that happened was hard for me too. For years, I dealt with my own internal conflict on a daily basis, struggling with feelings of regret and remorse over my actions and the pain I caused others, including you. I was tormented at the thought that this was my legacy—a messy and fractured life full of perversion and missteps. I shielded you from a lot of it, but I cried my share of tears as I worked through it all. With each onion skin layer that God peeled away, I felt the emotions and had to release them to Him. I made peace with God first before needing to make peace with others that I sinned against. You're a beautifully sensitive soul, Gin. That's part of why I fell in love with you to begin with. You feel deeply and need to work through things in your own time. I guess I have a little thicker skin than you do, and that's not meant as a dig at you. We're just different and deal with things in our own unique ways. Those things happened, Ginny, but it's not who you are. I'm proud of you for working through all this. I've seen you struggling but haven't known how to help you. I love the letter Abba gave you. So, just keep doing what you're doing. Feeling the pain, then releasing it to Him. Every day choosing to lay it all down. And freedom will come."

"Do you really still struggle with things, Sam?"

"Of course I do. Every now and then—like when I was looking through our wedding album and saw the picture of me with Willow and Aidan—I am reminded of my past and all the terrible mistakes I've made and the damage I've done, and it fills me with disgust and anger. But then I'm reminded that God doesn't hold it against me any longer, and I'm filled with hope again—just as you will be. It just takes time."

"Sam?"

"Mmm, hmm?"

Virginia paused for a minute, unsure how to proceed. "I really struggled over the years with feelings of hurt and betrayal over being the *other woman* in the affair and then the victim of your sexual objectification early into our marriage. I didn't know how to tell you how much it affected me, and I know I've lashed out in anger or closed myself off at times to you. But I'm just now understanding the reasons why. I'm sorry, Sam. Can you just be patient a while longer as I work through it all?"

"As long as it takes, Gin. I'll be here."

They sat there for a few more hours, talking and crying and laughing before retiring to bed for the night. It was a time of much-needed healing for Virginia as they held each other in the quiet hours. She fell asleep in Sam's arms and rested peacefully at last.

❁ ❁ ❁

The next day was Friday, and Virginia was excited to meet Miss Berti at the café, although she didn't think to ask if they were still meeting since it was right after Thanksgiving. She wanted to go into town anyhow to do a little shopping, so she would swing by regardless. She had so much she wanted to share.

Downtown was bustling with people going from shop to shop to get the big Black Friday deals. Virginia wished she had her flower shop ready for business to take advantage of all this foot traffic, but that was an unrealistic goal. She thought it more feasible to have a grand opening party after the New Year and start the year off with a bang. After visiting some of the stores, it was nearing 1:00 tea time at the Cinnamon Shack. Virginia was a little early, so she took a seat and decided to order some scones and tea while she waited for Berti.

"Hi, darlin'," Lois cheerfully said as she came over to the table to take Virginia's order.

"Hi, Lois. How was your Thanksgiving?" Virginia returned.

"Oh, it was great! Thanks for asking, Ginny. I usually have to do all the cookin', but it was at my sister's house this time, and she took care of it all. What a treat!" Lois said as she patted her belly. "And how about you? Did you have a nice Thanksgiving, hun?"

Virginia decided a little white lie wouldn't hurt in this instance, "Yes, thank you. It was lovely." Just then, the door opened, and in walked Berti. Perfect timing. "Oh, here's my Friday companion. Miss Berti! Over here!" she called out.

As Berti made her way over to the table and sat down, Virginia added, "I took the liberty to order some scones for us. Is that okay?"

"That sounds delightful," replied Berti.

"I was hoping we were still on for today. How are you, Miss Berti?"

"I am blessed, my dear, and thankful for another day."

"Speaking of thankful, how was your Thanksgiving?" Virginia asked.

"Oh, I had a really nice day. They make a big feast at the Community Center for Thanksgiving Day every year, and I always go there to help in the kitchen and enjoy the company of good friends, not to mention some good food."

"That sounds nice. I'm so glad for you. The Community Center seems like a wonderful place."

"Oh, it truly is. But, Ginny, I want to hear about your Thanksgiving. I believe you had some reservations about going to your cousin's house, was it?"

"Yes, well, it's Sam's cousin and his wife. It started out fine, but kind of went downhill from there." Virginia proceeded to tell Berti about the conversation she overheard and Leigh's disparaging comments. Then to further explain why it pushed her buttons so profoundly, Virginia finally told Berti the whole story of the Forbidden, from beginning to end and all the ugly in-between. She held nothing back as Berti listened intently and responded compassionately as the story unfolded with a soft gesture or word. Virginia was relieved to get it all out in the open and share it with someone so receptive and understanding, like Miss Berti. She wrapped up her story with her recent flashback and discussion with Sam afterward, then concluded by saying, "I know Abba wants me to be free from all the shame and regret, Miss Berti, but I'm struggling with how to let it all go."

"I can't imagine how difficult all that has been for you to carry around, Ginny. It's an incredible story."

"Hmm, I think you meant to say it's a *dis*-creditable story," Virginia said sarcastically.

"No. I meant to say *in*-credible. It's an incredible story of the real struggles of humanity and the unconditional love of God. It's an incredible redemption story. And you're right, Ginny; Abba desires your freedom from the tyranny of shame. You've been forgiven by God, by Sam's ex-wife, and by others it affected. But there's one person who hasn't forgiven you, Ginny."

Virginia looked at Miss Berti with uncertainty, "What do you mean, Miss Berti? Who?"

Berti took Virginia's hands in her own and, with the most loving tone, said, "You." She paused a moment to let it sink in. "There's a stumbling block in your life, Ginny. It's unforgiveness, mostly towards yourself. And until you can forgive yourself, and even Sam, for all that happened during those years of turning away, you'll continue to trip over that stumbling block. Early biblical writings call this a Skandalon. It's a trigger or a trap that causes us to stumble. It's where we get our word scandal, Ginny. And I know you understand that all too well."

Virginia didn't feel judged or looked down upon by Berti. Quite the contrary. She felt valued and uplifted. She knew the words Berti spoke were true, and while they stung as they pierced straight to the heart of the matter, they also carried a healing balm with them.

The café was getting crowded, and the noise level elevated, making it difficult to have this very intimate conversation in public.

"Ginny, why don't we pick up this conversation another time," suggested Berti.

Virginia looked around at the crowd of people, "I think that's a good idea. You've given me something to think about, though. Thank you for sharing that with me."

They motioned to Lois for their check and stood to leave. Virginia suddenly had an idea. "Miss Berti, instead of meeting here next week, would you be interested in coming with me next Saturday to Sam's winter outreach program at the village senior center? His students have been working so hard, and I think you would enjoy it."

"I would absolutely love that!" Berti exclaimed.

"Great! I'll see you then. It starts at 11:00 in the morning on Saturday. Do you need a ride?"

"No, thank you. I have transportation. I'll be there with bells on!"

CHAPTER 19

Show Time

December began fast and furious as final rehearsals and last minute preparations for the winter outreach program were in full swing. Virginia was volunteering as needed, in addition to getting all her ducks in a row for the Peace Rose Boutique's grand opening in January. On top of all that, Willow and Aidan were coming to stay for the week between Christmas and New Year's, and she wanted the house to be decorated and perfectly homey for their stay. A lot was happening all at once, but Virginia, as a high achiever, thrived in that environment, at least for a short while. She had to learn the right balance of activity and rest or she tended to burn out quickly. She would be the first to admit, though, that she hadn't mastered the balancing act yet, as sometimes it was all or nothing. And right now, it had to be all.

Virginia was carrying a few boxes of Christmas decorations from the garage when Sam caught her in the hallway. "Hey! There you are. Here, let me help," as he grabbed a box from the stack. "Gin, can I ask a big favor? I know you have a lot going on, but I was hoping you could help me out with something. After class tomorrow and before heading over to the village senior center to take care of some last-minute set and costume issues, I wanted to go visit Isaac's dad. He ended up serving some jail time and is permitted visitors now. I just really want to reach out to him. Anyhow, Isaac's mom has to pull a double shift at work and won't be home, and he's taking things a little hard with his dad's situation. I don't think it's a good idea for him to be home alone. Could he hang out with you for a while? Just a couple of hours, maybe?"

"Of course, he can! I was planning on going to the flower shop to do a little painting and check off a few boxes on my to-do list. But he can come along and help me if that's okay?"

"Oh, absolutely. I think he'd love to help. Thanks, Gin," he said as he gave her a peck on the cheek. "I'd be lost without you."

"Yes, you would," she laughed. She was actually looking forward to spending some one-on-one time with Isaac. Her heart went out to him for his troubled home life, and the promise of Isaiah 54:1 was burning inside of her.

The next day, Virginia and Isaac arrived at Peace Rose Boutique with a car full of items to take into the shop. She was so thrilled to see the sign hanging out front that she commissioned to be designed and installed.

"Oh, it's perfect! Absolutely perfect! Don't you think, Isaac?"

"It's pretty, Mrs. Sam."

"Yes, it is. It's so pretty. Now to make the inside just as pretty. I'll take these boxes in if you can carry that paint, okay? I'd love to finish touching up the paint inside today so I can start setting up the furniture, display racks, and plant stands. Then I can decorate. That's the really fun part."

Isaac helped to lay out the drop cloth and was in charge of keeping the paint tray full of paint while Virginia rolled it on the walls. He was also in charge of entertainment, as he loved to tell jokes.

"Hey, Mrs. Sam. Knock, knock."

"Who's there?"

"Pizza."

"Pizza, who?"

"You wanna pizza me? Huh?" Then, his infectious laugh filled the shop.

It wasn't long before the painting was complete, and Virginia unpacked the items she brought in from the car. Things were really beginning to shape up. Except for a dripping faucet in the bathroom, the shop's makeover was a success. Then after Sam's show, she would start decorating and filling the shop with beautiful floral arrangements.

"Isaac, before we stop for the day, can you hand me that toolbox over in the corner? I'd like to try to fix my faucet if I can. You know who was really good at this stuff?" she asked.

Isaac shook his head no.

"My Daddy. Daddy Grey could build and fix anything! He's my hero," Virginia smiled as memories of her dad coursed through her mind. Taking the pipe wrench, she tightened the plumbing connection to the faucet and whispered, "I miss you so much, Daddy."

"Where is he now?" Isaac asked.

"My Daddy? He's with my Mama in heaven. At home with God now, waiting for us to be with them again someday."

"I'm going to heaven, too," Isaac proudly announced. "But I hope my dad will be there like yours."

Virginia's heart sank. "Oh, sweetheart, I hope so, too. He's going through a hard time now, isn't he? And so are you. Let's keep praying for him, okay? Jesus will answer our prayers. I know it." Virginia reassured Isaac as she gently touched his arm. "What do you say we get out of here? Sam is going to meet us at the house, and then you two have a few last-minute preparations to take care of before the show on Saturday. I can't wait to see it!"

Isaac beamed with joy as he practically skipped out the door to the car. Then, once Virginia caught up to him, he called out, "Hey, Mrs. Sam! Knock, knock…"

❀ ❀ ❀

"It's show time!" Sam trumpeted in the room adjacent to the main recreational hall of the senior center. Finally, all of Sam's hard work and that of the students was about to be presented.

"Everyone, make a circle," he continued. "I'm so proud of each and every one of you for all the effort and dedication you put into practicing for today's show. I know it will be a blessing to all those who are in attendance. Remember, you don't have to be perfect. Just have fun. We're here to bless the residents and visitors of the village senior center. So, let's show them a good time, okay? Hands in the middle."

The students and volunteers all placed their hands in the center of the circle as Sam prayed, "Father, these kids are truly the joy of your heart. I ask that you help them today as they put on this show. And bless all who are here to support the outreach program. In your name, I pray…" and they all shouted, "Amen!"

Virginia met Berti at the entrance of the building, and they made their way to the second row, where Virginia had two seats saved. Within minutes, the activities coordinator of the center made her way to the front to introduce the production.

"Ladies and gentlemen, distinguished residents and guests, we welcome you to this year's special presentation brought to you by the Hopeland School District's Special Education Department. Refreshments will follow the presentation in the cafeteria. Now, please join me in giving a hardy round of applause for the Winter Wonderkids!"

Virginia laughed as she recalled when Sam and Isaac came up with that name. But it suited them. They were really wonderful kids, each and every one of them.

The show was a hit, as lines were delivered (sometimes with the assistance of volunteers off-stage), and dance numbers were performed. It was the perfect mix of humor and seriousness that reflected Sam's personality. And the kids gave their all. It was clear they were having a blast. The colorful props and fanciful costumes definitely grabbed everyone's attention. And when Isaac sang his song, there wasn't a dry eye in the room. It was truly a beautiful performance. Virginia was beaming with delight at their achievement.

As the imaginary curtain fell, those who were able rose to their feet and gave a standing ovation. The kids jumped and laughed and high-fived as they took it all in. When things settled down, Sam came over to Virginia and Berti.

Hugging Sam, Virginia said, "Oh, Sam, it was fantastic! I'm so proud of you, sweetie."

"Thank you," he replied. "The kids were amazing. Miss Berti, thank you so much for coming today. I've heard so much about you that I feel like I know you. What a pleasure to meet you," he said as he took her hand.

"It's so nice to meet you as well, Sam. What a beautiful performance! I enjoyed it so very much. Thank you for inviting me."

"Miss Berti, would you like to get a bite to eat in the cafeteria before you leave? They have quite the spread in there," Virginia inquired.

"Oh, my. I would love to, but I think I'm going to pass this time. It seems I'm not very hungry and I have a few errands to run yet today. But thank you. See you next Friday, Ginny?"

"Wouldn't miss it," Virginia hugged her, then walked her outside. She couldn't help but notice that Miss Berti looked a little pale and tired today. She hoped the drive over wasn't too much for her. She watched as she safely got into her car and then blew her a kiss and waved as she drove away.

The week following the big show was much calmer, and Virginia spent a lot of time at the shop organizing, decorating, and getting ready for her first shipment of flowers to arrive. Things were really beginning to take shape, and her vision was becoming a reality.

At home, the holidays were on full display as the last of the decorations were hung. After weeks of craziness, Virginia and Sam finally had some downtime and sat on the sofa while listening to soft, old-fashioned Christmas music playing in the background.

"When was the last time we just sat together like this?" Virginia asked.

"I can't remember. That's awful, isn't it!" Sam realized.

"Well, there's been a lot to take care of lately, but I'm glad it's settling down a bit now. The tree is beautiful. I love this time of year," Virginia said as she snuggled closer to Sam.

"Me, too, Gin."

They sat in the quiet a while longer enjoying the lights sparkle on the tree before Virginia spoke up. "Sam, I've been thinking. It's probably a long shot, but the kids are coming down at the end of the month, and I thought, wouldn't it be nice if Hannah and Lucas came down to visit, too? We could have a 'Nomad' family holiday in our new home."

"Nomad" was the mash-up name the kids came up with for Novak and Maddigan when referring to their "parental units," as they jokingly referred to them.

"Wow, really? I mean that would be great, but do you want to wait another year until we're really settled in? They've talked about wanting to come down to see the place eventually."

"Normally, I would say yes… to wait a little while, but for some reason, it feels right to ask now. I don't know."

"Well, it doesn't hurt to ask. I don't know if they have plans already, but I'll shoot them an email."

"Sounds good. If we plan a dinner party, I'd also like to invite a few others if that's alright with you. Like Miss Berti, Isaac and Maggie? Maybe Isaac's mom would like to come. I'd love to meet her."

"The more the merrier," Sam replied.

Virginia was excited at the prospect of having family and friends gather together in their new home. She placed her head on Sam's chest and savored the contentment she felt. Virginia was also excited to meet up with Berti the next day for their usual tea time. Because things had been so hectic lately, she actually hadn't given much more thought to where their previous conversation left off—Skandalon. Right now, that sounded too deep and complicated. She didn't want to ruin this peaceful moment all cozied up with Sam with the ambiance of Christmas surrounding her. For now, she would just sit with her love and simply be.

The next day, Virginia headed to the café to meet Berti. Normally, she would have loved the brisk walk into town, but the temperature was really dropping as mid-December was upon them, and since she had some other errands to run later, she decided to drive into town.

The cafe was more sparse than usual for a Friday afternoon, but she didn't give it much thought. If she had paid attention to the weather forecast, she would have known that a wintry mix was headed their way. She made her way over to their usual table and settled in to wait for Berti. Virginia noticed a couple of new paintings hanging on the wall that she hadn't seen before. One painting, in particular, caught her attention. With a bit of an abstract twist to a classic floral arrangement, the painting's calming palette of colors and movement of the brush strokes really captivated her. The assorted bouquet with hews of bluish-gray, purple, and green all flowing together cascaded from a slender white vase. It was truly beautiful. Lois interrupted her contemplation.

"Well, hi Ginny. You braved the cold today, I see. What can I get you, hun?"

"Oh, hi Lois. I think I'll have coffee today. Can you make a cappuccino?"

"Sure thing. Anything else?" Lois asked.

"Actually, I've been admiring that painting over there on the wall. Is it for sale?"

"Ah, yes. That's Amelia's creation. She's the owner's daughter who studies art abroad. She's really talented. I think it's for sale; let me check. Are you interested?"

"Yes, I am. I think it would be perfect for my flower shop. Let me know how much she's asking for it, and I'll pay for it when I leave. Thanks, Lois. By the way, is the time on that clock right? Berti's usually right on time or early. She's never been this late, so I'm kind of worried."

"Yep, that's the time, alright. Maybe it was too cold for her to be out and about today. Did she happen to give you a call?"

"No, she didn't. Maybe you're right. Hmm... I'll still take that coffee and wait a little while longer."

Virginia waited for an hour, but Berti never showed up. She didn't have her phone number but remembered that she spent a lot of time at the community center, and maybe they had her contact information. She decided to drive by there on her way home after she took care of some other errands and business matters before it got too late. On her way out of the Cinnamon Shack, she settled up with Lois and purchased the lovely artwork for the boutique. She knew the perfect place to display it. As she walked to the car, admiring her new treasure, she grew increasingly worried about Berti. *"Maybe she lost track of time. She's probably at the community center right now. I'm sure she's fine. I hope..."*

CHAPTER 20

Berti's Swan Song

Virginia rushed to Hopeland General Hospital as quickly as possible. It was only five miles outside of town, but each mile felt like an eternity. The cold snap pushing through Hopeland was moving quickly, and the mix of sleet and freezing rain made the drive quite treacherous. But Virginia was determined to get to the hospital to be by Berti's side – no matter what obstacle she faced!

Virginia's pulse was racing as she followed the signs to Visitor Parking. Slipping and sliding across the lot, she safely made her way to the hospital entrance and up to the front desk. She realized at that moment that she didn't even know Berti's last name. How shallow of her not to ask, she thought. Berti practically knew everything about her because she took the time to find out. She genuinely wanted to know. She asked. She listened. *"And I was so self-centered I didn't even bother to ask what her full name is,"* she thought, embarrassed at her lack of consideration. The front desk staff was kind enough to see past her flurried state, however, and in a calming and reassuring manner, located the patient and provided Virginia with Berti's room information.

How could someone who was a perfect stranger just two and a half months ago have burrowed so deeply into her heart? She felt a lump forming in her throat as she walked down the hallway, and pausing for a moment before pressing the elevator button to the fourth floor, she took a deep breath and whispered a prayer for strength.

As the elevator door opened and Virginia began to walk toward Berti's room, the sounds, smells, and bright, stark walls flooded Virginia's mind with memories. Difficult memories of doctor visits, long hours in waiting rooms, sleepless nights in uncomfortable bedside chairs, cafeteria food, and bad coffee. Oh, and those endless hospital noises—all of which she could hear clearly now—beeps and alarms from medical equipment, the hissing of respirators, footsteps, and conversations in the hallway. But worst of all... the sound of nothing after her loved one laboriously breathed her last breath. Silence.

Virginia bitterly recalled the heart-wrenching journey with her mom as she struggled with her lung disease. Her five-year struggle with pulmonary fibrosis was filled with pendulum swings of laughter, then tears. During those years, Virginia tried to stay hopeful and positive for her mom's sake, but all the while, feeling the impending threat of loss choke her optimism. Virginia's gate slowed to a mere shuffle as memories continued to flood her mind.

Finally, Virginia rounded the corner of the hallway to Room 403. Her head down and her thoughts a million miles away, she nearly plowed over the nurse who had just come out of Berti's room.

"Oh, I'm so sorry. My mind is somewhere else." She wiped her teary eyes. "Are you okay? Did I just step on your foot?" she asked as her face became flush with embarrassment.

"It's okay. I'm fine." The other woman smiled with an overwhelmingly compassionate radiance.

"Are you Berti's nurse?"

"Yes, I'm Grace. And, aside from being in a hurry, you are?"

Virginia timidly smiled at Nurse Grace, whose eyes were sparking with amusement. "My name is Virginia Novak. I'm a friend of Berti's. Is it alright if I visit with her for a while?"

"Yes, but just for a little while. I just checked her vitals, and she is very weak. She may slip in and out of sleep, but you're welcome to sit by her bedside if you'd like. I'll be here until 7:00 this evening if you need anything."

"Thank you so much." Virginia turned to walk into the room, but not before glancing back to the nurse to remark, "And next time, I'll watch where I'm going."

Grace chuckled while nodding her head, then continued down the hall, heading back to the nurses' station while humming a friendly little tune.

There she was. Hooked up to those noisy monitors and annoying tubes. Her eyes were closed, and her breathing seemed labored. Since meeting in the park that autumn day, Virginia always viewed Berti as being such a strong woman. And during the past few months, she was exactly that—a pillar of strength. But at that moment, she looked so frail and helpless. Not wanting to disturb her rest, she took a seat on the chair next to the hospital bed and compassionately watched over her… quietly praying and thinking about all that had transpired since she first met Miss Berti.

A few short minutes passed before Berti slowly opened her eyes, seemingly aware that someone else was in the room.

"Hi, Miss Berti. It's Ginny," she said as she gently took her hand. "Are you in any pain?"

"No. Whatever cocktail they have pumping in me seems to be doing the trick," she snickered as she attempted to raise her arm slightly to show the IV.

"Oh my! Yes, I see. Thank goodness for that! You had me worried, Miss Berti. You missed our tea date. I thought maybe you finally got tired of listening to me ramble on about my life's saga," she teased.

"Never, my child. I'd never grow tired of your company. But it seems like my heart is getting tired of ticking. At least that's what the doctors are saying."

"Now, don't trouble yourself with that right now. You've been through quite an ordeal, haven't you!"

Berti took a very deep and intentional breath and then proceeded to explain the events that led to her hospital visit. "Well, I went to the market to get some walnuts. I wanted to make a batch of my nut rolls for my friends at the community center. You know, I make them every year around Christmas. I felt a bit of a dizzy spell in the parking lot, but I just brushed it off and got what I needed from the store. Then I went back home and took a little nap 'cause I was feeling so tired. I felt a little better after about an hour, so I made my cookies and headed over to the community center. I wanted to make sure they had them for the holiday. But when I got there, I felt really strange and had a sharp pain. Apparently, I fell in the parking lot. I don't remember exactly. But some nice fella who was volunteering at the center saw me and called 911. They say I had a heart attack, Ginny."

"Oh my, Miss Berti! I'm so glad that man was there to help you! I wish I would have known sooner. I would have come right away."

"I know, Ginny. But you're here now. That's all that matters."

Berti's voice was growing faint and trailed off a bit as her eyes closed, and she began to drift to sleep again. Virginia's heart broke at the helplessness she felt. She wanted so desperately to be able to take Berti home, out of that dreary hospital room, make her comfortable, and take care of her.

Her thoughts were interrupted by the sound of her phone vibrating in her purse. She was glad she remembered to turn it on silent mode before coming into the hospital so she didn't disrupt Berti's rest. Moving to the other side of the room, she softly answered.

"Hello?"

"Hey, Gin. Babe, where are you? I came home, and the house was empty."

"Oh, I'm so sorry, Sam. I forgot to leave a message for you. I'm at Hopeland Hospital."

"What!! Are you okay?"

"No, no. It's not me. I'm fine. It's Miss Berti. She had a heart attack, Sam. I went to the community center to ask if they knew where she was because she missed our weekly tea date. They told me about rushing her to the hospital, and I jumped in my car and drove straight here. I just reacted and forgot to call you."

"It's fine. I was just a little worried. Is Berti okay now?"

"I don't know yet. She seems stable but very weak. She's resting now, and I'd like to stay with her for a while. Is that alright with you?"

"Of course, Gin. Do you want me to come over too?"

"No, it's okay. I'm just gonna sit with her for a bit. I'll call you when I'm headed home."

"Alright. Sounds good. I love you, Ginny. I know you've grown fond of Miss Berti. I'll be praying, and if you need anything at all, call me. And be careful out there. The roads are slick."

"I know. I will. Thanks, Sam… I love you, too."

Virginia placed the phone back in her purse and stood at the window, watching the wintry mix continue to fall outside. She watched as the lights along the sidewalk began to shine like candles against the frosty ground. It was so serene-looking and beautiful, and for a moment, she forgot where she was. Virginia looked over at Berti and uttered a prayer under her breath. "God, please hold Miss Berti in your arms right now. Give her peace."

About half an hour passed before Berti awakened once more. This time, she abruptly opened her eyes, and her body jolted as if she were startled by something.

"Berti, it's okay. I'm here. Are you alright? Do you need the nurse?"

"No. No. I don't want the nurse. Ginny, I need to talk to you."

"Miss Berti, maybe you should just rest some more. We can talk later when you are feeling up to it."

"No, it's important. I need to talk to you now, child. Please sit next to me."

Virginia sat in the chair next to Berti's bed, handed her a cup of water, and waited patiently for Berti to take a sip. It took a while for her to get situated before speaking, but when she began, her eyes flew wide open and fixed upon Virginia with sparks of intensity firing from them.

"My dear Ginny. I don't have much time left, so I need to share something with you before it's too late…"

"Now, Berti! Don't…" Virginia protested at the use of the phrase *before it's too late*.

"Please let me finish," Berti interrupted. "I know my time is short, and I'm at peace with that. Really, I am. But it's important you hear me out." Berti's eyes were blazing with purpose now as Virginia eased back into the chair and nodded her head in submission.

"I have lived a full life—one filled with many ups and downs and with many lessons learned along the way. For the most part, I have learned what it means to be content and happy despite the circumstances. I'm honored that you've shared so much of your story with me these past few months. But I've been somewhat close-lipped about my own life. I think it's time I told you a few things."

Berti's expression turned sober for a moment as the images of days gone by flashed through her mind like a slideshow.

"Things were hard when I was a young girl. A lifetime ago, really! You know, Ginny, my birthday is next month, and I'm no spring chick anymore!"

A thin, sarcastic smirk formed on Berti's mouth as she once again caught Virginia's gaze. Ginny smiled in response, wondering where this was all headed. After taking another sip of water, Berti began to share her story.

Bertha Kotnik, born in the early '30s in Yugoslavia (present-day Slovenia), never knew her birth parents and bounced around between grandparents, aunts, and even strangers until such time she was placed in an orphanage at age 6. For years, Berti suffered cruelty and abuse by the orphan keepers... presumably due to her stuttering problem and left-handed tendencies while writing or drawing. This was considered unacceptable by her orphanage tutors, as they would forcibly restrain her left hand or smack it with a wooden stick if Berti resisted. Then whacked her in the head if, while attempting to protest, Berti stuttered words in opposition. This mistreatment continued for many years.

World War II was soon ravaging the country, compelling the children and house "mothers" to evacuate the orphanage through Hungary to Vojvodina, in the northernmost part of Serbia. These were very harsh and perilous times, as Berti recollected the hunger and exhaustion she felt as they tried to find refuge. Berti's childhood was fraught with many abuses—physical, psychological, and even sexual. By the tender age of 14, she was on her own and made her way to Hungary, where she, a gadji (non-Romani), was accepted into the Roma community. Though considered the gypsy slums, Berti found a sense of home and belonging for the first time in her life. It was there she found God... and it was there she met her husband, Andrew Nagy.

Andrew Nagy was a Hungarian whose father emigrated to America when Andy was just a young boy. His father was working to save money in order to bring the rest of his family across the sea to be reunited once more. Meanwhile, Andy, the young adolescent—now, man of the house—found whatever work he could to help support his mother and young sister until they could join his father in America. Berti met Andy in a small village outside of Budapest, and the young man's keen sense of humor immediately charmed Berti. It didn't take long before the two were inseparable, and upon turning 18, Andy asked for Berti's hand in marriage.

Berti continued to share more details of her story. She told of the economic difficulty she faced as a newlywed migrating from Hungary to America. The high expectations each brought into their marriage that neither could satisfactorily fulfill. The horrific events surrounding her abuse as a child and how she believed it to be the link to her inability to conceive a child. The shunning she received from the small-town community because of her ethnicity and impoverished upbringing. The crude insults hurled at her— "filthy gypsy"—as she walked the streets, acts of vandalism to her home, and even threats of bodily harm.

The muscles in Virginia's hands began to tighten as Berti's story unfolded. She couldn't bear to think of this precious lady enduring such horror... such pain.

"I'm so sorry, Miss Berti. I can't even imagine what you went through." Virginia gently squeezed Berti's hand in an attempt to somehow ease past hurt.

"No need to be sorry, my dear. I dealt with these things long ago. But the point I am trying to make is that for so many years, I carried unforgiveness and resentment deep in my heart. It was planted there as just a child, and upon each instance of abuse, its roots grew deeper and deeper. Until all I saw was hate. I hated the people who were supposed to take care of me but instead only hurt me. I hated my enemies whose war brought young predators to our village who exploited the innocence of children. I hated those who abused and mistreated me; yes, it's true. But I hated myself too."

"What are you talking about!" Virginia exclaimed. "None of that was your fault! You were just a child!"

Before Virginia had a chance to protest, Berti raised her hand. "I know. I know that's not true. I understand that now after all these years. But at the time, shame somehow convinced me I was to blame. What I'm trying to say, my dear Ginny, is that to practice forgiveness, even towards ourselves, is one of the greatest gifts of all. It's the key to our true healing and freedom."

A tear rolled down Virginia's cheek onto the side rail of the hospital bed. Berti was the wisest woman she had ever met.

"We didn't get the chance to finish our conversation from the café a couple of weeks ago. Remember when I told you about that word, Skandalon?"

"Yes, of course. I remember Miss Berti."

"When I first met you, I could see it in your eyes—the shame and unforgiveness. We are very much alike, Ginny. Our own personal scandals have caused stumbling blocks in our lives at one time or another. I have grown so fond of you these past few months, and I don't want it to trip you up any longer, Ginny. You have a wonderful life ahead of you."

Virginia's tears fell in droves now. She couldn't have fought them back if she tried. The dam of her soul was wide open at the truth-filled words of Berti and the tenderness with which she spoke. The unselfishness of this precious woman was astonishing. Here she was on the hospital bed, barely clinging to life. Virginia should have been the one comforting her; instead, in her final hour, Berti was comforting Virginia.

Minutes passed in silence. The lump in Virginia's throat kept her from uttering a single word. And Berti's strength was slowly slipping away. Virginia broke the silence with a quivered whisper, "Berti, I… I don't know how…" Her voice trailed off into sobs.

"How to forgive yourself?" Berti finished the sentence. Virginia nodded.

"Raise my bed, will you dear?"

"What? Are you sure, Berti? No, you need to just rest. I should go and let you get some sleep." Virginia wiped her face and tried to gain composure.

"Please."

Virginia could sense the quiet urgency in Berti's single plea. She took the hand control from the bedside table and raised Berti's bed, lifting her head so she was in a reclined seated position.

Berti's voice was feeble and broken. "It's not always an easy road, but trust me, it's worth the effort. Abba will help you. Make a choice every day to walk the road of forgiveness. And before you know it, you'll be soaring with wings of freedom, far above the Skandalon below." Berti looked over at the side table to where a few personal items sat. She motioned to Virginia as she spoke, "See that ring there? Can you pick it up?" Virginia did what was asked of her. "That ring means a great deal to me. It symbolizes the covenant I have with My Beloved One, my Savior, Yeshua. It's been a reminder to me all my life that I belong to him, and with every passing day, to do all I can to make myself ready for his return."

Virginia opened Berti's hand to place the ring in her palm. But Berti handed it back to Virginia, "I want you to have it, Ginny. I have no children of my own to pass it on, but you have become like a daughter to me, a spiritual daughter, and it would mean so much to me if you kept it as a reminder. He is coming for his pure, spotless Bride, and you are part of that, Ginny."

Virginia accepted the gift and, through cascading tears, sniffled and uttered, "I'm honored, Berti. Thank you." Berti would have no idea the significance of her gift, as Virginia recalled her spiritual encounter so many years ago regarding the Heart of the Bride. "I will treasure this precious gift always," she added.

Berti's face suddenly brightened, and her eyes grew wide as her gaze shifted upward. Virginia could hear her whisper, "My Beloved." Berti smiled and reached out her hand to touch Virginia's wet cheek. "Oh child, you are so loved. He has made everything beautiful in its time." At that, her hand dropped to her side, and she exhaled her final breath.

Virginia collapsed into Berti's lap and wept uncontrollably, unaware of the drone from the flatlining heart monitor or the rush of hospital staff entering the room. It wasn't the bustling around her that stirred Virginia from her mournful state. But suddenly, the scent of magnolia flowers filled the room. She instantly understood it was a supernatural sign from God, Berti's Beloved, who just received her into His arms.

Nurse Grace compassionately placed her hand on Virginia's shoulder as the monitors were powered off and tubes removed from Berti's spiritless body. Virginia looked up at Nurse Grace, smiled through her tears, and gently spoke, "Do you smell that? It's the fragrance of magnolias. A symbol of purity and beauty. Miss Berti is home."

CHAPTER 21

Letting Go

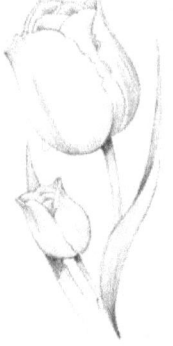

Virginia was astounded at how one person could impact her life so drastically in only a couple of months. She was filled with so much grief at the loss of her friend, her spiritual mother figure. The fingerprints of Berti's life were everywhere, as constant reminders of her surfaced throughout the day. She opened up to Sam about the series of events that occurred at the hospital.

"Sam, you should have seen her. She was so selfless and caring even to the end. And she was so much at peace and confident in where she was going. The only thing she seemed to care about was getting a message to me," Virginia sobbed. "And there is still so much I don't know about her. Oh my word, her story, Sam... her story was heartbreaking yet so filled with hope. I've never met anyone like her in my entire life. I miss her so much..." she trailed off.

"I know, Gin. She was so very special. I'm just glad you had that time with her. I'm so sorry, hon." Sam held Virginia tightly in his arms to try to ease her sorrow. "How can we find out what her wishes were and what arrangements will be made?"

Virginia wiped her eyes, "I'm not really sure. She didn't have any family, but maybe the community center will know. I'll call them tomorrow. Sam, I'm really tired and think I'll go lie down a bit, okay?"

"Of course. Get some rest. And don't worry about anything. I'll take care of dinner tonight."

Virginia collapsed in the bed with a box of tissues in hand. The ache of missing Berti, as well as her parents, was so palpable. She hugged her pillow and cried until she finally dozed off for a little while. Upon waking, the words of Berti were forefront of her mind. *When we first met, I could see it in your eyes—the shame and unforgiveness... Make a choice every day to walk the road of forgiveness. And before you know it, you'll be soaring with wings of freedom, far above the Skandalon below... He has made everything beautiful in its time.*

Virginia sat up in bed and hung her head in dismay. She couldn't believe Berti was gone. She finally found someone who she trusted to confide the hidden secrets of her life... someone who listened without judgment and imparted hope and words of wisdom... and now, she was taken away. Virginia wrestled with feelings of anger and hurt at the sudden loss, but in her reasoning, she knew Berti was completely whole and filled with joy upon her homecoming. Virginia just wished their time together wasn't so brief. She wished a lot of things in the stillness of that quiet bedroom. She wished Berti was going to be at the Cinnamon Shack next week; she wished her parents were still alive to share her new adventures in Hopeland; she wished she never Turned Away and took the wayward road of the Forbidden. She could feel herself being sucked back into her usual coping mechanisms of shutting down and becoming numb. Even after so many years had passed, the anxiety associated with being the "other woman" imprinted indicators of trauma upon her life. She still felt the intensity of the emotional, physical, and spiritual symptoms of trauma associated with the affair and suicide attempts. But now, she had a choice to give in to the triggered patterns or shatter them with her next course of action.

Virginia mulled over the past few months spent with Berti. From their first encounter at the park, sitting on the bench together, to the happenstance meeting at the café after her flashback while standing in the rain. The encouraging note about being a spiritual mother to many, and words of wisdom about the power of self-forgiveness. There were so many precious moments, and Virginia rehearsed them all.

She walked across the bedroom and grabbed the Bible from her writing desk. Opening to the book of Ecclesiastes, she read from chapter 3, verse 11.

He has made everything beautiful in its time.
He has also set eternity in the human heart;
yet no one can fathom what God has done
from beginning to end.

Virginia certainly couldn't fathom why God allowed everything that happened in her life. *In its time...* She reread that line. She realized it had been fourteen years that she struggled with forgiving herself, as well as forgiving Sam for the part he played. For all those years, she desired to be free of the shame, hurt, and resentment she carried inside and to move on with her life, but for some reason, she couldn't find her way through it all. Yet somehow, God used Berti's words to form a key that unlocked the prison doors of her soul. Their relationship opened a deeper level of understanding for her and now, she could see clearly the Skandalon that was tripping her up all this time.

Virginia, finding comfort in reading the scriptures, turned a few more pages in her Bible and fell upon another verse that grabbed her attention. *"The end of a matter is better than its beginning."* Could it be that God was fashioning a story of her life, a love letter of sorts, wherein the beauty of its ending was being forged from the ashes of the dawn of her Turning Away? — The weight of its glory far outshining the ruins of her past.

Virginia felt like she was at a point of no return, where her next choice would determine the course of her life. After taking time to ponder all the conversations, memories, and messages over the past couple of months, things began to make sense. What she had viewed as her worst enemy—her past and the Forbidden—wasn't her enemy at all. Unforgiveness was the enemy of her soul, robbing her of joy and freedom. She didn't know how Abba would work it all out, but she made a decision at that moment to offer herself the same grace, mercy, and kindness that she extended to others. To choose to walk the road of self-forgiveness every day. She also made a choice to release Sam from his past role of betrayer and objectifier. She knew he was acting out from his own hurts and struggles, and inasmuch as she no longer wished to be subjected to past sins, she no longer wanted Sam to be enslaved to former transgressions. She desired to put a pin in the ballooning monster of shame, let go of her past, and embrace the restored innocence of her true identity, Virginia Abigail—Pure Joy.

As Virginia verbalized this revelation in the form of a prayer and petitioned the Lord to set her free from the bondage, she took a deep breath and could feel a weight lift from her chest. She gave thanks to Abba for his gift of forgiveness, for his redemption, his freedom and for the blessing of knowing Berti even for just a short time. Her life would be changed forever. The story of redemption was being written upon her heart by the Master Poet.

Sam quietly opened the door and entered the bedroom. "Hey Gin, how are you feeling?"

"Better, thank you," she smiled at him, and instead of eyes of sadness, she had a glimmer of hope in them.

"Good. I made a little something to eat if you're hungry."

"Actually, I'm not very hungry tonight. I'm sorry you went to the trouble."

"No trouble at all. It'll be okay to heat up tomorrow if you want." Sam sat next to her on the bed. "Well, are you ready for this?"

Virginia just looked at him with curiosity.

"Hannah and Lucas replied to my email."

"And?" Virginia probed.

"They want to come down. They can't make it a long trip but would like to come down at the end of the month for a few days and leave right after the New Year. Does that work?"

"Perfect. We'll celebrate the New Year together as one big, happy, blended family," she chuckled.

"Who would have thought," Sam joined in.

"Certainly not me, but apparently God did. Well, I have some planning to do then. Let's throw a New Year's Eve dinner party!"

Christmas was soon upon them, and both Sam and Virginia agreed to make it a special, quiet day—just the two of them. Aside from making a few phone calls to family, the kids, and friends up north wishing them a Merry Christmas, they made Virginia's favorite holiday dish, stuffed cabbage, then baked cookies and ate them while watching classic Christmas musicals, such as White Christmas and Holiday Inn. It was the perfect, nostalgic

Christmas Day. The sense of sadness at loved ones who had passed away and were no longer with them during the holidays was still very much felt by both, but there was an accompanying peace and comfort, knowing that where they were was far better. Virginia didn't want to dampen the mood but wanted to tell Sam of her findings.

"I called the community center, and they told me that there's no funeral service planned for Miss Berti at her request. She'll be buried at Hopeland Cemetery, but the folks at the center want to have a memorial for her after the New Year. I think that would be nice. They'll send me more details when it's all planned out."

"Okay, sounds good. Your grand opening is coming up, too. Are you getting excited?" Sam asked.

"I am looking forward to it. I think I have the place ready. I just need to take care of a few more things and make sure I have enough product, but for the most part, yes. I can't believe it's happening! I'm looking forward to getting to know some of the other shop owners on the street and to build my clientele."

"You're amazing, Ginny. I'm so proud of you. I thought this the very first time I met you and I still think that you're just full of surprises," Sam kissed his bride.

"Well," Virginia responded, "You'll be even more surprised at what I'm about to say next."

"Oh? You have my attention."

"I think we should also invite Mick and Leigh to our New Year's dinner."

"Um… Okay? Now, that *is* surprising to hear. Are you sure about that? After the Thanksgiving debacle?"

"That was pretty bad," Virginia moaned. "Maybe I'm a glutton for punishment, but I want to give it another chance. Mick has been so kind to us, and even though Leigh has her own issues to deal with, I think I'm in a better frame of mind to handle her now."

"Well, if you're sure, I'm okay with it. But she'll be in our home, Ginny. One hurtful word, and I'll tell her to leave." Sam said sternly.

Virginia cupped his face in her hands, "My hero!"

Sam smiled at that but said in a more serious tone, "I mean it, Gin."

Then, affectionately kissing him, Virginia responded, "I know, sweetie. Thank you. The kids will be here in a couple of days and they can help me to go shopping and get ready for the party. Meanwhile, one more movie before we call it?"

"My Brother the Time Traveler?" Sam immediately blurted out with excitement.

"Yeeesss!" Virginia jumped up and ran to the DVD player.

After picking up Willow and Aidan at the airport and spending a few days of quality time with them, catching up on college stories and school gossip, and showing them around town, including

Virginia's new shop, the Peace Rose Boutique, New Year's Eve dinner was the next focus of attention. Hannah and Lucas got into town the night before and were staying at a bed and breakfast a few minutes away. The Nomads were all together again.

During prayer time one morning, as part of Virginia's devotional time and daily choosing the way of forgiveness, she had an idea for a gift she wanted to give Hannah. She found exactly what she wanted and ordered it online. Upon returning home after picking up some party supplies with the kids, the package was on the doorstep.

"Oh, yay! My package arrived. I was a little worried it wouldn't come in time. Hey guys, can you take the bags of groceries from the car into the kitchen for me? I want to take care of something quick."

Willow and Aidan jumped right on their task, yelling for Dad to come out and help them, of course. Virginia grabbed the package and bolted upstairs. Opening the box and removing the protective wrap, she saw the painting she ordered, and it was perfect. A picture of white tulips on a dark background. Further inspecting it to make sure it was not damaged in shipment, she placed it next to her desk, sat down, and, taking a pen and paper, began to write a note.

Dear Hannah,

I've been on a journey lately, one that is many years overdue, but that was first put in motion by you. Your bravery in walking the path of forgiveness and releasing me from the offense of my actions set a course of events in motion for me to forgive myself and others. Through God's merciful workings, and with the help of a very precious friend recently, I am finally experiencing the freedom that comes with forgiveness. As a symbol of my gratitude, I wanted to give you this gift. White Tulips have a meaning of forgiveness, purity, innocence and honor. So, please accept this painting as a portrait of our story of redemption and forgiveness.

Merry Christmas,
Ginny

She folded the note and placed it inside a Christmas card, sealed it in an envelope, and then, after wrapping the painting, attached the envelope to the gift with ribbons and a bow. Virginia felt so liberated, so full of gratitude and joy in that moment. She carried the gift down the steps and placed it under the Christmas tree, along with a few other unopened gifts for her party guests.

The "Nomad" New Year's Eve party was proving to be a huge success. In attendance were eleven in total: Hosts Sam and Virginia, along with Willow, Aidan, Hannah, Lucas, Mick, Leigh, Maggie, Isaac, and Isaac's mom, Sarabeth. Miss Berti's absence was privately unmistakable, but Virginia wore the ring Berti gave her on a chain around her neck and would periodically hold it in her hand as a point of connection and remembrance. Only Sam knew what that gesture meant.

Virginia's burgundy beef stroganoff, prosciutto-wrapped asparagus, and stuffed mushrooms were a hit, although Sam avoided the mushrooms like the plague, for he was not shy in expressing his distaste for the fungi. Dessert and champagne cocktails followed as guests congregated in the family room to enjoy conversation and games. Maggie's boisterous laugh echoed throughout the house as she was clearly enjoying the title of Charades champion. And Isaac entertained with the occasional knock-knock joke.

"Knock, knock."

"Who's there?" Everyone rang out in unison.

"Isaac."

The room once more echoed, "Isaac, who?"

Then Isaac delivered the punchline as he dramatically threw his hands up in the air, "*I sick* of knock-knock jokes!"

The fun, laughter, warmth, and love in the Novak home that evening were abundant. Apart from Leigh's inability to look Virginia in the eyes, she held her tongue from making any snide remarks the entire time. Leigh was unusually quiet and spent most of the time observing those around her.

As soon as Virginia sensed the appropriate time, she began to hand out the gifts she had for her guests. Each one of them had something either created or bought by Virginia. Gifting wasn't normally one of her love languages, but she enjoyed finding things that were unique or had special meaning to the recipient—case in point, Hannah's gift.

Hannah opened her present and read the note. "Oh my word, Ginny." Tears welled up in her eyes, "this is the most thoughtful and beautiful thing I've ever received." Then turning to her husband, Lucas, made a clarifying statement. "That is, apart from you, babe." Everyone laughed as Lucas grinned and shook his head as he rebutted, "Good save, Han."

Hannah and Virginia embraced as tears flowed freely from almost everyone in the room. Sam lightened the mood by announcing, "It's almost midnight, everyone! Let's turn on the TV and watch the ball drop!"

Virginia couldn't have been more pleased at the success of her gathering. She was so happy they decided to have the party at this time. The guests all departed, except for Isaac, who had permission to stay the night at the kids' request, as the Novaks tidied up the kitchen before going to bed. But little did Virginia know that the evening's events were not quite finished.

Mick and Leigh were on their way home. Even Mick thought it odd that his wife was so quiet, as normally she would be chattering away, perhaps criticizing something at dinner or remarking on someone's outfit. But Leigh sat in the passenger's seat as quietly as a church mouse. Mick spoke up.

"Everything okay, Leigh? You're awfully quiet this evening."

"I don't know. I'm just deep in thought, I guess," she replied rather timidly.

"About anything in particular? Did something upset you tonight?" Mick continued his inquest.

"Don't you think it's just weird how Ginny and Hannah are all buddy-buddy? I don't get it. If I were Hannah, I'd never have anything to do with her after everything she did!"

"Well, it's obvious that they've both reconciled and resolved their feelings about the situation. Hannah is very outspoken about her process of forgiving both Ginny and Sam. She gives all the credit to God for healing the trauma associated with the affair and then restoring to her an amazing marriage with Lucas. I like him. He's a cool guy," Mick added as a side note.

"They just all get along so well. And the kids. They seem happy. I just don't understand." Leigh was desperately searching for some reasoning behind what she just encountered at the Novak's home. There was not one ounce of animosity or awkwardness. But only an atmosphere of peace and love, acceptance and respect, positivity and joy. Leigh just couldn't wrap her head around it all.

Mick interjected his thoughts on the matter. "Leigh, do you think you're having trouble with their situation because you've never forgiven your father for what he did to you and your family?"

"What do you mean I haven't forgiven my dad?" Leigh snapped. "Of course I have! It's been over thirty years. I'm over it!"

"Doesn't sound like it," Mick responded. Leigh sneered back at him. "Sorry, I didn't mean to upset you," he continued. "It's just that all the things you say about Ginny and the way you treat her… if you don't have any issues, then it doesn't really add up. Do you recall ever really talking with your dad about everything? I mean, do you remember *when* you forgave him?"

His words shot through Leigh like an arrow through the heart. While she felt enraged at his line of questioning, she started to consider that maybe there was truth to what he said. Maybe she never resolved the issues surrounding her father's extramarital affair and his subsequent abandonment of the family. *"That's ridiculous,"* she thought. *"Of course, I've forgiven him."* But the more she thought about his comments, the more she realized that he was right. *"Why do I treat Ginny that way?"* she asked herself. *"What did she ever do to me personally?"* Leigh became quietly introspective. These new revelations caused a lump to form in her throat. She began to tremble, and, for the first time in many, many years, Leigh began to cry. After a few minutes, she cleared her throat and impulsively spoke up.

"Mick, turn around."

"What?"

"Stop the car and turn around. We need to go back."

"Where? Back to Sam's? We're almost home! Did you forget something?"

"No. Please, just turn around… NOW!" she forcefully insisted.

Mick, a little confused, complied and turned the car around to go back to the Novak's home.

Virginia had just wiped down the kitchen countertop and was outing the kitchen light to head up to bed when she heard a slight knock at the door.

"Who in the world could that be at this hour?" she mumbled to herself. Looking through the peephole of the door, there stood Leigh. Baffled to see her again, Virginia opened the door.

"Leigh? Is everything okay?" She could tell Leigh had been crying from the red eyes and smudged makeup.

"Ginny, can I talk to you for a minute? I'm sorry it's so late." Leigh's demeanor was different. While obviously upset about something, she wasn't on the offensive or cheeky. She seemed somewhat humble.

"Of course, come in. Is Mick here with you?"

"He's gonna stay in the car."

"Okay," Virginia said with a tinge of perplexity. "Here, have a seat. Do you want a drink?" Virginia's hospitality was still in high gear.

"No. Look, Ginny, you know me. I'm a straight shooter, so I'm just gonna come out with it. I want to tell you..." she paused. "I... I'm... oh, I don't know what I'm doing here!" Leigh recoiled. "I just can't make sense of anything."

Leigh was groping for the words to describe what she was feeling inside but was coming up short.

"Look, I guess it's no secret that I've held a grudge against you for years. And you know why."

"Yes, I know," Virginia politely acknowledged.

"And... I..." again, Leigh paused to search for the words. Virginia remained quiet.

Seeming more frustrated now, Leigh grumbled, "Why is this so hard!?"

Virginia, sensing Leigh's exasperation, tried to ease her by saying, "Leigh, it's okay. You don't have to say..."

"No, I do! That's the point. What I have to say, Ginny, is that... I'm sorry! I'm sorry for being so mean to you over the years. But seeing you and Hannah together tonight did something in me. And I don't understand it. Even after all the hurt, you are friends and even spend the holiday together! I mean, who does that!?"

At that statement, Virginia laughed. "True. I guess that's not the norm for most people in these situations."

"How did you do it? Get past it all? You all seem so carefree and at peace." Leigh's edginess began to soften now.

"It's taken a very long time, Leigh. But God has done an amazing work of healing and restoration in all of our lives."

"Mick thinks that I've never dealt with the issues with my father and that I've projected those feelings onto you."

"And what do you think?" Ginny inquired.

"I don't know. I thought I had, but I guess I haven't. After all, he…" Leigh now began to break down.

"He hurt you by his betrayal, didn't he? I'm so sorry that happened to you, Leigh. And I'm sorry that my past mistakes have been a source of contention for you. Sam and I have both acknowledged the fact that what we did was wrong, and as a result of our choices, people were hurt. We've since reconciled and have made peace in our situation, but the effects of our actions were much farther-reaching than I thought." Virginia took Leigh's hand.

Leigh was sobbing uncontrollably now. But through her sobs, she uttered, "I'm sorry, Ginny. I'm so sorry for how I've treated you."

Virginia comforted her, "It's okay, Leigh. It means a lot to hear you say that. Look, you may not want to confide in me because of what I represent, and that's alright, but if you ever need to talk about what happened to you or what you are going through now, please know that I am always here. You may think of me as the other woman based on what you went through, but I'm not your enemy, Leigh. Maybe God can use pieces of my story to help you heal."

Leigh shook her head. "I have a feeling we'll be talking a lot more in the days to come."

"It's an amazing new start for a promising New Year!" Virginia declared.

The two hugged for the first time in all the years they had known each other. As Virginia closed the door behind Leigh, she turned, leaned back on the door, and shook her head.

"*Unbelievable!*" she thought. "*Thank you, Abba. I never could have imagined that the key to seeing such miracles would be in my letting go…*"

CHAPTER 22

New Beginnings

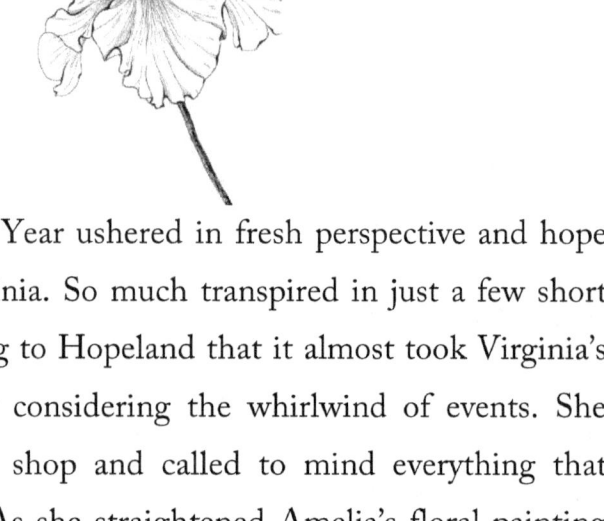

The New Year ushered in fresh perspective and hope for Virginia. So much transpired in just a few short months since moving to Hopeland that it almost took Virginia's breath away, simply considering the whirlwind of events. She stood in her flower shop and called to mind everything that happened recently. As she straightened Amelia's floral painting that she bought at the café, which now hung proudly on her shop wall, she thought about the day she first saw the place. "It's exactly how I imagined it would be," she quietly uttered.

The blush pink and soft gray paint colors on the walls created the perfect backdrop to highlight the assortment of plants and flowers throughout the shop. The vintage off-white highboy dresser was the perfect addition to showcase a variety of vegetation. She opened a few of the dresser drawers to creatively house some vining plants that rose, then cascaded from the drawer towards the floor. The ornate, oval-shaped distressed mirror that hung on the wall above the dresser was a classy addition.

Virginia took in every detail, from the crimson pink and cream drapery to the variety of display tables and stools exhibiting the array of flowers, including gerbera daisies, calla lilies, snapdragons, and orchids. She took a minute to sit down at the small white scroll metal table in the corner of the room and voiced her heartfelt sentiments towards heaven.

"Mama, I wish you were here with me. Maybe God would allow you to peer through an opening in heaven just to see this place… our place—The Peace Rose. Here's to a brighter future, Mama."

She sat for a few moments longer before hearing the bell on the front door jingle. Sam entered. "Excuse me, ma'am, but do you know where I can buy some flowers?" he grinned from ear to ear. "Your first and *favorite* customer is here." He greeted Virginia with a kiss, then continued, "Seriously, Ginny. This is amazing. I can't believe how you transformed this old place. You've truly outdone yourself!"

"You're so sweet. But I do love how it all turned out." Then Virginia took Sam on the grand tour. "Right now, what you see is the front shop where all the transactions will take place, but check this out. Phase two will be back here. I envision revamping this back room into a cool place where people can congregate in a relaxing atmosphere—plants and flowers everywhere, of course—

and have a cup of tea or coffee while they meet with a friend or read a book in a comfy chair, maybe over there in the corner." Virginia became animated as she glided from one side of the room to the other, describing to Sam what she visualized.

"Then I'd like to convert this back door into a set of French doors to a patio out here," Virginia continued as she escorted Sam outside. "It's perfect for an outdoor garden area, don't you think? We can hold mini-concerts for local musicians and host workshops and support groups. Oh! And maybe a men's group that you can share your story with to help them through their struggles. It would be perfect because it's so private back here." Virginia said as she winked at Sam.

"I can even envision small 'church' gatherings," she used air quotes to emphasize church. "You know, like we used to talk about. Connecting with our community and sharing life as we pursue God together. There's so much potential here, Sam."

Sam's smile enlarged. "I haven't seen you this happy and excited about something in a long time, Gin. It's a good look for you."

Virginia turned her head away slightly and smiled. He could still make her blush after all this time. But he was right. She was happy and filled with creativity and hope for the future. She even felt a spark reignited within her when she mentioned local musicians. Virginia could see herself singing and writing songs with Sam again. It seemed as though past dreams that were dormant for years began to awaken in her heart once more. She would just take it one day at a time.

Sam took one more walk around the shop. "I can see the potential here, too, Ginny. And I love your vision for it. All of it. Let's get phase one going tomorrow with your grand opening, and then, the sky's the limit!"

Sam put his arms around Virginia, then with a softer tone asked, "Are you ready?"

Nodding her head, Virginia answered, "Yeah. I need to get something first."

Virginia went to her workstation and retrieved the most beautiful silk flower arrangement of blue iris, white lilies, lavender, and lemon leaves.

"Beautiful," Sam commented. "I know you always have meaning behind what you create. So, what does the blue flower mean?"

"Well, the blue flower is an iris, and it represents the power of hope and the enduring nature of faith. That's Miss Berti through and through. The white lilies can symbolize purity, new beginnings, and hope. Those are all things that the Lord has been renewing in me over these past few months, in large part because of the time I spent with Miss Berti. So, I thought it fitting to include them in her bouquet."

"She'd love it. I'm certain of it."

Virginia and Sam drove to Hopeland Cemetery and located Berti's gravestone. On it was engraved a simple inscription: *Bertha Kotnik, Beloved Child of God.*

Virginia knelt down and placed her flower arrangement on Berti's grave.

"Thank you so much for coming into my life, Miss Berti. If only I could tell you how right you were about all of it. I'm just now starting to soar above the Skandalon below, and it's beautiful. I know I still have a long way to go, but I understand now. I owe so much to you." Virginia wiped the tears from her wet cheeks then continued, "I miss you so much. But I want you to know that I'm continuing our tradition at the Cinnamon Shack with Maggie and Leigh. Oh, my! If only I could tell you *that* story! But I will someday. I'll tell you everything when our Beloved calls us all together. One day, very soon."

Virginia rose to her feet and turned to hug Sam harder than ever. Upon showing their respect and saying their final goodbyes, hand-in-hand, they began to walk out of the cemetery. As they passed grave after grave, Virginia recalled her journal entry, R.I.P., and recent flashback of the cemetery during that very dark season in her life. But this time, as the memory emerged, it lacked the sting that it once possessed. It was the first time since the onset of the Forbidden that shame no longer had her in its cruel grip. Forgiveness was perfecting its work within her.

What once was the Scandal of Virginia Grey had now been redefined as the Redemption of Virginia Novak.

"White Tulip" painting by Sharon Crane (used by permission).

About the Author

Wendy Crane is the author of *The Scandal of Virginia Grey*, a fiction based on true events. Wendy's primary occupation for over 30 years has been as a legal and administrative assistant. To satisfy her creative bent, however, Wendy has been involved in music in one way or another most of her life. As singer/songwriters, Wendy and her husband, Maurice (Reese) Crane, both individually and jointly, have released several albums, including *Letting Go* in 2010. Whether through their band, Creekside Soul or as worship leaders within the church, Reese and Wendy continue to use their gifts to glorify God.

As founders of The Silent Addiction, Reese and Wendy Crane have an intense desire to attend to the needs of those who have suffered deep wounds in the area of sexual addiction and extramarital affairs. Because of their story of sex addiction, infidelity, deceit, emptiness, and brokenness, as well as forgiveness, healing, freedom, restoration, and reconciliation, they are very well-equipped to rescue others in the same struggle. Their heart is to see the sex addict, the other woman, and the betrayed spouse all find healing in the arms of a loving Father and Bridegroom who will bring peace and rest to a weary and wounded soul.

Wendy and her husband reside in Florida near the Gulf Coast where she, a true aquaphile, can satiate her love of the water.

https://www.thesilentaddiction.com/scandal-book.html